Certification Study Companion Series

The Apress Certification Study Companion Series offers guidance and hands-on practice to support technical and business professionals who are studying for an exam in the pursuit of an industry certification. Professionals worldwide seek to achieve certifications in order to advance in a career role, reinforce knowledge in a specific discipline, or to apply for or change jobs. This series focuses on the most widely taken certification exams in a given field. It is designed to be user friendly, tracking to topics as they appear in a given exam and work alongside other certification material as professionals prepare for their exam.

More information about this series at https://link.springer.com/bookseries/17100.

Dynamics 365 Business Central Developer Certification Companion

Hands On Preparation for the MB-820 Exam

Dr. Gomathi S

Apress®

Dynamics 365 Business Central Developer Certification Companion: Hands On Preparation for the MB-820 Exam

Dr. Gomathi S
Microsoft Most Valuable Professional,
Microsoft Certified Trainer,
Microsoft Learn Expert
Coimbatore, Tamil Nadu, India

ISBN-13 (pbk): 979-8-8688-0925-5 ISBN-13 (electronic): 979-8-8688-0926-2
https://doi.org/10.1007/979-8-8688-0926-2

Copyright © 2024 by The Editor(s) (if applicable) and The Author(s), under exclusive license to APress Media, LLC, part of Springer Nature

This work is subject to copyright. All rights are reserved by the Publisher, whether the whole or part of the material is concerned, specifically, the rights of translation, reprinting, reuse of illustrations, recitation, broadcasting, reproduction on microfilms or in any other physical way, and transmission or information storage and retrieval, electronic adaptation, computer software, or by similar or dissimilar methodology now known or hereafter developed.

Trademarked names, logos, and images may appear in this book. Rather than use a trademark symbol with every occurrence of a trademarked name, logo, or image we use the names, logos, and images only in an editorial fashion and to the benefit of the trademark owner, with no intention of infringement of the trademark.

The use in this publication of trade names, trademarks, service marks, and similar terms, even if they are not identified as such, is not to be taken as an expression of opinion as to whether or not they are subject to proprietary rights.

While the advice and information in this book are believed to be true and accurate at the date of publication, neither the authors nor the editors nor the publisher can accept any legal responsibility for any errors or omissions that may be made. The publisher makes no warranty, express or implied, with respect to the material contained herein.

    Managing Director, Apress Media LLC: Welmoed Spahr
    Acquisitions Editor: Smriti Srivastava
    Development Editor: Laura Berendson
    Editorial Assistant: Kripa Joseph

Cover designed by eStudioCalamar

Distributed to the book trade worldwide by Springer Science+Business Media New York, 1 New York Plaza, Suite 4600, New York, NY 10004-1562, USA. Phone 1-800-SPRINGER, fax (201) 348-4505, e-mail orders-ny@springer-sbm.com, or visit www.springeronline.com. Apress Media, LLC is a California LLC and the sole member (owner) is Springer Science + Business Media Finance Inc (SSBM Finance Inc). SSBM Finance Inc is a **Delaware** corporation.

For information on translations, please e-mail booktranslations@springernature.com; for reprint, paperback, or audio rights, please e-mail bookpermissions@springernature.com.

Apress titles may be purchased in bulk for academic, corporate, or promotional use. eBook versions and licenses are also available for most titles. For more information, reference our Print and eBook Bulk Sales web page at http://www.apress.com/bulk-sales.

Any source code or other supplementary material referenced by the author in this book is available to readers on GitHub. For more detailed information, please visit https://www.apress.com/gp/services/source-code.

If disposing of this product, please recycle the paper

To my beloved mother, whose love and guidance have shaped every page of this book. Your memory and spirit continue to inspire me every day.

Table of Contents

About the Author xix

About the Technical Reviewer xxi

Acknowledgments xxiii

Introduction xxv

Chapter 1: Introduction to Dynamics 365 Business Central Development 1
Overview of Dynamics 365 Business Central Development Role 2
    Introduction to Dynamics 365 Business Central 2
    Integration and Customizations/Extensions 4
    Deployment Options 5
Key Benefits of Using Dynamics 365 Business Central 5
    Increased Efficiency 5
    Improved Decision-Making 6
    Scalability 7
    Enhanced Collaboration 8
Overview of Dynamics 365 Business Central Development Role 9
    Core Responsibilities 9
    Scenario: Implementing a Custom Sales Report 11
    Impact on Business Efficiency 12
Responsibilities of a Business Central Developer 12
    Designing and Architecting Solutions 12
    Coding and Implementation 13

Table of Contents

- Quality Assurance and Debugging 13
- Deployment and Maintenance 13
- Collaboration and Communication 14
- Certification Learning and Improvement 14
- Scenario: Upgrading an Existing Business Central System 15
- Checklist for the Roles and Responsibilities of a Business Central Developer 16

Introduction to AL Language and Its Significance 18
- Why AL Language? 18
- Uniqueness of AL Language 19
- Comparison with Other Languages 19

Overview of Development Tools and Environments 20
- Introduction to Development Tools 20
- Business Central Sandbox Environment 21
- Source Control Systems 22
- Deployment Tools 22
- Scenario: Developing and Deploying a Custom Module 23

Conclusion 23

Key Takeaways 24

Exercise 26
- Analyzing the Benefits of Business Central 26

Exercise Solution: Analyzing the Benefits of Business Central 26
- Key Challenges Faced by XYZ Manufacturing Before Implementing Business Central 27
- How Business Central Helped Address These Challenges 28
- Benefits Experienced by XYZ Manufacturing Post Implementation 29

TABLE OF CONTENTS

Chapter 2: Installation, Development, and Deployment for Business Central Chapter 31

Managing Sandbox Environments 32

AppSource Submission 33

Prerequisites 33

Getting Started with Visual Studio Code for Business Central Development 34

    Installation 34

    Features of Visual Studio Code 34

    Extensions in Visual Studio Code 34

    Getting Started with Visual Studio Code 35

    Using AL Language in Visual Studio Code 35

Installing the AL Language Extension in Visual Studio Code 36

    Installation Steps 36

    Post Installation 37

    Testing and Debugging Your Application 37

    Using Docker Images for Upcoming Releases 38

    Managing Prerelease Versions 38

    Actual Steps for Installation and Configuration 39

Discovering the Logical Database and Its Objects 47

    Core Object Types 47

    Extending Business Central 48

    Logical Database Structure 49

    Object Numbering Conventions 49

    Managing Objects 50

    General Rules 50

Development Process: Designing, Developing, and Testing Solutions 50

    Designing Solutions 50

ix

TABLE OF CONTENTS

Deployment Strategies for Business Central Apps 53
    1. Preparing for Deployment 53
    2. Using AL Extensions 54
    3. Managing Versions and Updates 55
    4. Multitenant Deployments 56
    5. Postdeployment Activities 56
    6. Rollback Strategy 57
    Tips for Successful Deployment 57
    Deployment Strategies Checklist for Business Central Apps 58
Segment AL Code and Reduce Naming Conflicts with Namespaces 62
    Declaring Namespaces 62
    Using the Namespace Keyword 63
    Example of Namespace Declaration 63
    The Using Directive 63
    Nested Namespaces 64
    Managing Namespaces and Object Names 64
    Practical Tips for Namespaces 64
    Integration with Microsoft Power Platform Products 65
    Integration Checklist for Microsoft Power Platform Products 69
    Postintegration Activities 74
Conclusion 74
Key Takeaways 75
Exercise 76
    Exercise 1: Setting Up a Sandbox Environment 76
    Exercise 2: Building a Simple Extension 77

Chapter 3: AL Object Development in Business Central 79

    Introduction to AL Programming 81

        Types of AL Objects 81

    GitHub Copilot 128

    Conclusion 129

    Key Takeaways from This Chapter 130

    Exercises for Chapter 3: AL Object Development in Business Central 132

        Exercise 1: Create a Table... 132

        Exercise 2: Create a Card Page 132

Chapter 4: Working with Development Tools in Business Central 137

    Overview of Development Tools for Business Central..................................... 138

        Introduction 138

        Visual Studio Code... 139

        AL Language.. 139

        Business Central Extension 139

        Azure DevOps 140

        Docker 140

        PowerShell 140

        Standalone Development Environment 140

        AL Test Runner.. 141

        Business Central Administration Center 141

    Utilizing Development Environments Effectively in Business Central............... 141

        Introduction 141

        Types of Development Environments 142

        Best Practices for Environment Management 142

        1. Version Control 142

        2. Continuous Integration/Continuous Deployment (CI/CD) 143

TABLE OF CONTENTS

    3. Environment Parity 144

    4. Data Management 146

    5. Access Control 147

    6. Monitoring and Logging 148

    7. Documentation 148

    Effective Use of Docker for Local Development 150

    Sandbox Environment Strategies 150

    Production Environment Considerations 151

    Case Study: Streamlining Multienvironment Development at
TechnoGlobe Inc 151

Debugging and Troubleshooting Techniques in Business Central 153

    Introduction 153

    1. Using the Debugger in Visual Studio Code 153

    2. Logging and Tracing 155

    3. Error Handling 156

    4. Performance Profiling 157

    5. Telemetry and Monitoring 159

    Case Study: Troubleshooting a Complex Integration Issue 160

Performance Optimization Strategies in Business Central 163

    Introduction 163

    1. Code Optimization 163

    2. Query Optimization 165

    3. Caching Strategies 167

    4. Background Processing 168

    5. Application Design Considerations 171

    Case Study: Optimizing a Large-Scale Inventory Management System 173

TABLE OF CONTENTS

Business Central-Specific Performance Tools and Considerations
for MB-820 179
    1. Performance Toolkit for Microsoft Dynamics 365 Business Central 179
    2. Database Performance Optimization 180
    3. AL Performance Best Practices 181
    4. Cloud Performance Considerations 182
    5. Performance Testing for Extensions 184
    Case Study: Optimizing a Complex Business Central Extension 186
    Exercise 1: Debugging and Optimizing AL Code 190
    Exercise 2: Implementing Telemetry and Performance Testing 192
Solutions 195
Solution for Exercise 1: Debugging and Optimizing AL Code 195
    Solution for Exercise 2: Implementing Telemetry and Performance
    Testing 197
Conclusion 204
Key Takeaways 204

Chapter 5: Integration of Business Central with Other Applications 207

Comprehensive Guide to Business Central Integration Methods 208
    1. Power Apps with Business Central 208
    2. Power Automate with Business Central 210
    3. REST Services in Business Central 211
    4. Azure Functions with Business Central 212
    5. Web Services in Business Central 213
    6. Business Central API 214
    7. Shopify and Dynamics 365 Business Central (D365BC) 214
    8. Power Pages 216

TABLE OF CONTENTS

Understanding Integration Scenarios and Requirements for Business Central 217
- Introduction 217
- Common Integration Scenarios 217
- Key Requirements for Integration 218

Detailed Case Study: E-commerce Integration for Worldwide Traders 219
- Company Background 219
- Integration Scenario: Business Central and Shopify Integration 220
- Detailed Integration Requirements 220
- Integration Solution Architecture 223
- Challenges Faced and Solutions 227
- Outcomes and Benefits 228
- Lessons Learned 229

Integration Techniques and Methods for Dynamics 365 Business Central 230
- Introduction 230
- 1. APIs (Application Programming Interfaces) 230
- 2. Web Services 231
- 3. Power Automate (Microsoft Flow) 232
- 4. Power Apps 234
- 5. Azure Functions 235
- 6. Event-Driven Architecture 236
- 7. Batch Processing 237

Data Synchronization and Consistency in Business Central Integrations 238
- Introduction 238
- Key Concepts 239
- Synchronization Methods 239
- Ensuring Data Consistency 241
- Handling Synchronization Failures 243

TABLE OF CONTENTS

Best Practices for Data Synchronization and Consistency 244

Case Study: Implementing Robust Data Synchronization 245

Best Practices for Seamless Integration with Dynamics 365 Business Central 246

1. Thorough Planning and Analysis 246

2. Robust Architecture Design 247

3. Efficient Data Management 248

4. Security and Compliance 249

5. Performance Optimization 250

6. Testing and Quality Assurance 251

7. Documentation and Knowledge Management 252

8. Continuous Improvement 253

9. Governance and Support 254

Checklist for Business Central: E-commerce Integration Design 255

1. Integration Method Selection 255

2. Architecture Design 255

3. Data Synchronization Strategy 255

4. Security Considerations 256

5. Performance Optimization 257

6. Error Handling and Monitoring 257

7. Data Validation and Integrity 257

8. Testing Strategy 257

9. Deployment and Maintenance 258

10. Documentation and Training 258

11. Compliance and Legal Considerations 258

12. Future-proofing 258

13. Best Practices Implementation 259

TABLE OF CONTENTS

Conclusion 259
Key Takeaways 261
Exercise 263
    Solution 263

Chapter 6: Exam Preparation and Practice 265
Overview of MB-820 Exam Objectives and Structure 266
    Exam Objectives 267
Exam Structure 268
    Preparation Considerations 269
Study Strategies and Resources for MB-820 Exam 270
    1. Create a Study Plan 270
    2. Leverage Official Microsoft Resources 271
    3. Utilize Third-Party Resources 271
    4. Hands-On Practice 272
    5. Join Community and Discussion Forums 273
    6. Effective Note-Taking and Review 274
    7. Stay Updated 274
MB-820 Exam: Practice Exercises and Sample Questions 275
    1. Describe Business Central 275
    2. Install, Develop, and Deploy for Business Central 276
    3. Develop by Using AL objects 276
    4. Develop by Using AL 277
    5. Work with Development Tools 278
    6. Integrate Business Central with Other Applications 278
Tips for Exam Day Readiness: MB-820 Microsoft Dynamics 365
Business Central Developer 279
    1. Pre-exam Preparation 279
    2. On Exam Day 280

TABLE OF CONTENTS

    3. During the Exam 281

    4. After the Exam 283

    5. Post-exam Steps 283

    Conclusion 284

  Key Takeaways 285

Index **287**

About the Author

Dr. Gomathi S is a Microsoft MVP, MCT, and Microsoft Learn expert with more than 13+ years of experience as a technical trainer. She is passionate about educating urban students and specializes in Power BI, Business Central, and Azure AI. Known for her engaging webinars and training sessions, Dr. Gomathi covers a range of topics, including Azure AI Vision, Power BI, Tableau, Python, Power Apps, and Business Central. She authored the Apress book *Mastering Microsoft Dynamics 365 Business Central: A Comprehensive Guide to Successful Implementation* and mentors through the Code Without Barriers program. Her educational YouTube content, including video series such as *AL Coding Carnival* and *Business Central Chronicles*, aims to advance knowledge in emerging technologies and tools.

About the Technical Reviewer

Enrico Lisk focuses on leveraging technology to drive business innovation and efficiency, helping clients navigate the complexities of digital transformation in business applications, data, and AI. He has an impressive experience of 10+ years as a CIO in the apparel and finance sector and 15+ years in IT consulting. He is well versed in Dynamics 365, Sage, Oracle NetSuite and Dynamics CRM, Azure ML/AI, Power Platform, and LLM technologies. He currently serves in the capacity of Director Digital Transformation at ZILLIONe Technologies.

As a non-executive director (volunteer) at STEMUp, Sri Lanka, Enrico promotes the adoption of STEM education in schools across Sri Lanka.

His other technical reviews include *Mastering Microsoft Dynamics 365 Business Central* by Dr. Gomathi S.

Acknowledgments

With profound gratitude, I honor my father, V. Srinivasan, and my husband, Anantha Krishnan A., whose unwavering support has been the bedrock of my journey.

To my twin gems, Vishanth A. and Vishwant A., your boundless joy illuminates my life.

I extend my heartfelt thanks to Lakshmi V. and Appadurai K., my cherished in-laws, whose encouragement has been a guiding light.

To Mahalakshmi and Padmanaban, who resemble the warmth and love of my parents, your presence has been a comforting embrace.

I am also deeply grateful to my brother, Mr. Viswanathan S., and my sisters-in-law, Gomathy S. and Anantha Kalyani A., for their unwavering support and love.

I will always cherish the love and support of my friends Indira, Dhivya Prabha, and Krithika.

A Special acknowledgment goes to my CEO of Atna Technologies India Pvt Ltd., Gopalakrishnan and my role-model Srividhya Subramony, Vice President whose trust in me has wellspring of inspiration.

Finally to Sowmya Thodur and Smriti Srivastava, your prompt and insightful guidance from proposal to publication has been invaluable.

All your collective support and love have been the wings beneath my aspirations.

Introduction

In today's rapidly evolving business landscape, organizations are increasingly turning to robust, integrated business management solutions to streamline their operations and drive growth. Microsoft Dynamics 365 Business Central stands at the forefront of this digital transformation, offering a comprehensive platform that combines enterprise resource planning (ERP) capabilities with modern cloud technology. As businesses adopt this powerful tool, the demand for skilled developers who can customize, extend, and integrate Business Central to meet specific organizational needs has never been higher.

Dynamics 365 Business Central Developer Certification Companion: Hands On Preparation for the MB-820 Exam is your definitive guide to mastering the intricacies of Business Central development and achieving Microsoft certification. This book is meticulously crafted to provide aspiring and current developers with the knowledge, skills, and practical experience needed to excel in their roles and pass the MB-820 exam with confidence.

Throughout this comprehensive guide, we will embark on a journey that covers all aspects of Business Central development, from foundational concepts to advanced techniques. Each chapter is designed to build upon the previous, creating a solid framework of understanding that aligns perfectly with the MB-820 exam objectives.

We begin by introducing you to the world of Dynamics 365 Business Central development, outlining the roles and responsibilities and the significance of the AL programming language. From there, we delve into the practical aspects of installation, development, and deployment processes, ensuring you have a robust understanding of the entire development lifecycle.

INTRODUCTION

As we progress, you'll gain in-depth knowledge of AL object development, mastering the creation and modification of various object types while adhering to best practices. We'll also explore the essential development tools at your disposal, honing your skills in debugging, troubleshooting, and performance optimization.

Recognizing the importance of connectivity in modern business solutions, we dedicate a chapter to integration techniques, teaching you how to seamlessly connect Business Central with other applications and ensure data consistency across your systems.

Finally, we conclude with a focused exam preparation chapter, providing you with strategies, resources, and practice exercises to ensure you're fully prepared for the MB-820 certification exam.

Whether you're an experienced developer looking to validate your skills, a newcomer to the Business Central ecosystem, or a professional aiming to advance your career, this book serves as your comprehensive companion. With hands-on examples, practical insights, and exam-focused content, you'll not only prepare for certification success but also gain the real-world skills needed to thrive as a Dynamics 365 Business Central developer.

Embark on this learning journey with us, and unlock the full potential of Dynamics 365 Business Central development. Your path to certification and professional excellence starts here.

CHAPTER 1

Introduction to Dynamics 365 Business Central Development

This chapter serves as an essential starting point for understanding the role and responsibilities of a Dynamics 365 Business Central developer. It introduces the fundamental concepts of Business Central development, providing insights into developers' daily tasks and duties. You'll learn about the significance of the AL Language in creating custom solutions and how it empowers developers to enhance Business Central functionality. Additionally, the chapter covers the essential development tools and environments, offering a comprehensive overview to set you up for success in your development journey. By the end of this chapter, you'll have a clear picture of what it takes to be a proficient Business Central developer, equipped with the knowledge to build effective solutions.

CHAPTER 1 INTRODUCTION TO DYNAMICS 365 BUSINESS CENTRAL DEVELOPMENT

Overview of Dynamics 365 Business Central Development Role

Introduction to Dynamics 365 Business Central

Dynamics 365 Business Central is a comprehensive business management solution designed to streamline and automate business processes across various departments within an organization. Developed by Microsoft, this ERP (enterprise resource planning) system integrates multiple functionalities, including finance, operations, and sales, into a single, unified platform as shown in Figure 1-1.

> **Tip** Microsoft has recently announced new AI-driven features for Dynamics 365 Business Central to further enhance automation and efficiency!

Key Features

1. **Financial Management**: Business Central offers robust financial management capabilities, allowing organizations to manage their financials with precision. Features include general ledger, accounts payable and receivable, bank reconciliation, and fixed asset management. These tools enable accurate financial reporting and ensure compliance with regulatory standards.

CHAPTER 1 INTRODUCTION TO DYNAMICS 365 BUSINESS CENTRAL DEVELOPMENT

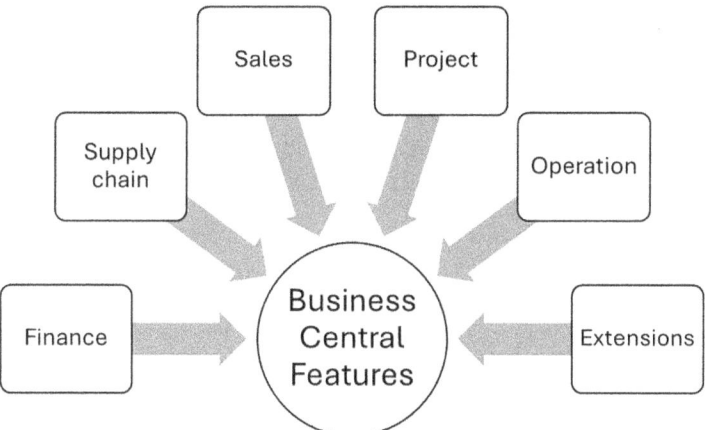

Figure 1-1. *Business Central Features*

2. **Supply Chain Management**: The platform provides comprehensive supply chain management features to optimize inventory levels, manage purchasing processes, and maintain vendor relationships. This helps businesses reduce costs, improve procurement efficiency, and ensure timely delivery of goods and services.

3. **Sales and Service Management**: Business Central integrates sales and service management functionalities, enabling organizations to manage customer relationships effectively. This includes lead and opportunity management, sales order processing, and service order management, helping businesses enhance customer satisfaction and drive sales growth.

4. **Project Management**: With Business Central, organizations can manage projects efficiently from start to finish. The solution offers tools for project planning, from resource allocation, to budgeting, and tracking progress, ensuring projects are completed on time and within budget perspective.

5. **Operations Management**: Business Central streamlines operations management by providing tools for production planning, manufacturing, and warehouse management. This ensures that production processes are efficient, inventory levels are optimized, and orders are fulfilled accurately and promptly.

Integration and Customizations/Extensions

One of the standout features of Dynamics 365 Business Central is its seamless integration with other Microsoft products, such as Office 365, Power BI, and Azure. This integration enhances productivity and collaboration by allowing users to work within familiar interfaces and leverage powerful analytics and cloud services.

In addition to Microsoft's ecosystem, Business Central supports third-party integrations through add-ons available on the Microsoft AppSource. These add-ons, created by various partners, extend the functionality of Business Central, allowing businesses to customize the platform to meet their specific needs. For example, ZILLIONe has published several add-ons, which can be explored at `https://appsource.microsoft.com/en-us/marketplace/apps?search=zillione&page=1`. These integrations provide

CHAPTER 1   INTRODUCTION TO DYNAMICS 365 BUSINESS CENTRAL DEVELOPMENT

tailored solutions that can enhance various business processes, offering users the flexibility to adapt Business Central to their unique operational requirements.

Additionally, Business Central is highly customizable. Organizations can tailor the platform to meet their specific business needs through extensions/customizations. The use of AL (Application Language) enables developers to create bespoke solutions that enhance the core functionalities of Business Central.

Deployment Options

Dynamics 365 Business Central offers flexible deployment options, including cloud and on-premise. This flexibility allows organizations to choose a deployment strategy that aligns with their IT infrastructure, security requirements, and budget considerations.

Key Benefits of Using Dynamics 365 Business Central

Increased Efficiency

Dynamics 365 Business Central is designed to streamline business processes, automating repetitive tasks and reducing manual data entry. This leads to significant time savings and allows employees to focus on more strategic activities:

- **Automated Workflows**: With built-in workflows for common business processes, Business Central reduces the need for manual intervention. For instance, automated invoicing and payment processing can save hours of administrative work each week.

- **Integrated Operations**: By integrating various business functions, such as finance, sales, and inventory, into one platform, Business Central eliminates the inefficiencies and errors associated with using multiple disparate systems. This integration ensures that data flows seamlessly across departments, providing a unified view of the business.

Tip Companies using Dynamics 365 Business Central have reported up to a 40% increase in operational efficiency within the first year of implementation!

Real-World Example: A mid-sized manufacturing company implemented Business Central to automate its inventory management and order processing. This resulted in a 30% reduction in order fulfillment time and a 20% increase in overall operational efficiency.

Improved Decision-Making

Business Central provides comprehensive data analytics and reporting capabilities, empowering organizations to make informed decisions based on real-time insights:

- **Real-Time Data Access**: With Business Central, decision-makers have access to up-to-date information across all business functions. This real-time access to data enables more accurate forecasting and quicker responses to market changes.

- **Advanced Reporting and Analytics**: The platform includes robust reporting tools and integrates seamlessly with Power BI Pro license, allowing users to create detailed reports and interactive dashboards. These tools help in identifying trends, monitoring performance, and making data-driven decisions.

Real-World Example: A retail chain used Business Central to consolidate sales data from multiple stores into a single dashboard. This allowed management to identify best-selling products and optimize inventory levels, leading to a 15% increase in sales and a 10% reduction in stockouts.

Scalability

Dynamics 365 Business Central is built to scale with your business, accommodating growth and evolving business needs without requiring significant changes to the system:

- **Flexible Deployment Options**: Business Central offers both cloud and on-premise deployment options, allowing businesses to choose the model that best fits their needs. As the business grows, it can easily switch to a different deployment model or scale up the existing one.

- **Modular Design**: The platform's modular design enables organizations to add new functionalities and users as needed. Whether it's expanding to new markets, adding new product lines, or increasing the workforce, Business Central can adapt to these changes smoothly.

Real-World Example: A fast-growing e-commerce company started with Business Central's basic modules for finance and sales. As the business expanded, they gradually incorporated additional modules for inventory management and customer service. This modular approach allowed them to scale their operations efficiently without disrupting ongoing activities.

Enhanced Collaboration

By integrating with other Microsoft products like Office 365, Business Central enhances collaboration and communication within the organization:

- **Seamless Integration with Office 365**: Employees can use familiar tools like Outlook, Excel, and Teams directly within Business Central. This integration streamlines workflows and fosters collaboration by enabling users to share information and work together more effectively.

- **Unified Platform**: Having a single platform for all business processes ensures that all team members are on the same page. It reduces miscommunication and ensures that everyone has access to the latest data and insights.

Real-World Example: A professional services firm integrated Business Central with Microsoft Teams, allowing project managers to collaborate with their teams more effectively. This integration led to better project tracking and a 25% improvement in project delivery times.

Dynamics 365 Business Central offers numerous benefits, including increased efficiency, improved decision-making, scalability, and enhanced collaboration. By integrating various business functions into a single, cohesive platform, it enables organizations to operate more smoothly and respond quickly to changing business environments. Real-world examples demonstrate how businesses across different industries have leveraged these benefits to achieve significant operational improvements and drive growth.

Overview of Dynamics 365 Business Central Development Role

The role of a Dynamics 365 Business Central developer is pivotal in tailoring the Business Central platform to meet specific business needs. Developers are responsible for customizing and extending the functionality of Business Central, ensuring it aligns with the unique processes and requirements of the organization. This involves designing, coding, testing, and deploying solutions that enhance the platform's capabilities.

Core Responsibilities

A Business Central developer's responsibilities encompass a wide range of activities as shown in Figure 1-2, including

- **Design and Architecture**: Developers design the structure of custom solutions, ensuring they integrate seamlessly with existing systems.

CHAPTER 1 INTRODUCTION TO DYNAMICS 365 BUSINESS CENTRAL DEVELOPMENT

- **Coding and Implementation**: Writing and implementing code using AL (Application Language) to create extensions and customizations.
- **Testing and Debugging**: Thoroughly testing customizations to ensure they work as intended and debugging any issues that arise.
- **Deployment and Maintenance**: Deploying solutions to production environments and maintaining them to ensure continued performance and relevance.

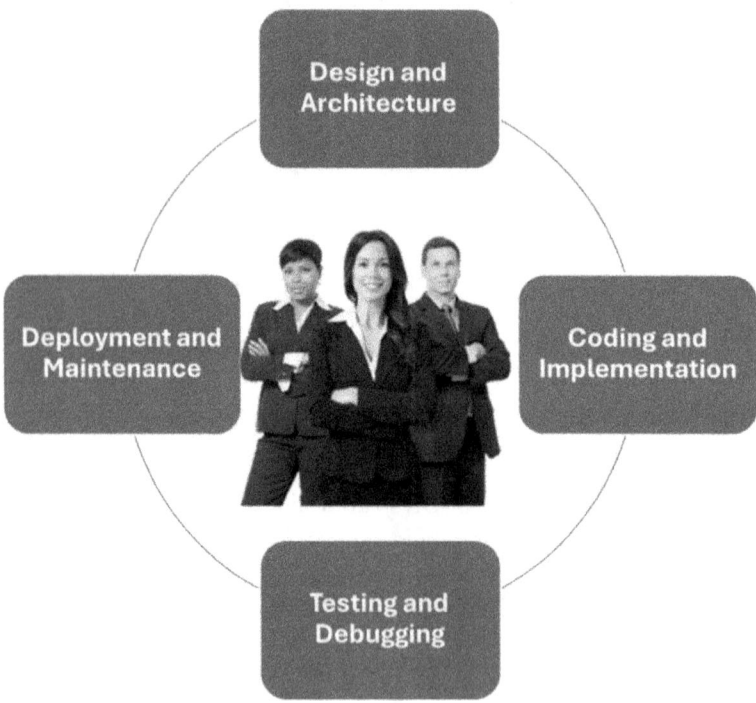

Figure 1-2. *Core Responsibilities (Source: This photo by unknown author is licensed under CC BY-NC.)*

CHAPTER 1   INTRODUCTION TO DYNAMICS 365 BUSINESS CENTRAL DEVELOPMENT

Scenario: Implementing a Custom Sales Report

Imagine a mid-sized retail company that uses Dynamics 365 Business Central to manage its operations. The company needs a customized sales report that includes specific metrics not available in the standard reports. The Business Central developer steps in to address this need:

1. **Requirement Gathering**: The functional consultant gathers the requirements, including specific metrics, business logic, and the desired output format for the custom report. They then prepare a functional requirement document.

2. **Design and Planning**: The functional consultant briefs the developer, who designs the report layout and determines how to fetch the necessary data from the Business Central database.

3. **Coding**: Using AL, the developer writes the code to create a new report object, pulling data from various tables and presenting it according to the specified format.

4. **Developer Testing**: The developer tests the report with sample data to ensure accuracy and makes any necessary adjustments.

5. **Functional Testing**: Following developer testing, a functional consultant conducts functional testing. This involves preparing test data and scenarios to ensure the report meets business requirements.

6. **User Acceptance Testing (UAT)**: After functional testing, the report undergoes user acceptance testing, where end users validate that it meets their needs and expectations.

7. **Deployment**: Once the report passes UAT, it is ready for deployment into the production environment.

In this scenario, the functional consultant plays a key role in translating business needs into detailed functional requirements. They collaborate closely with the developer, who then uses their technical expertise to implement these requirements as functional solutions within Business Central. Together, they ensure that the solution not only meets the business objectives but also enhances the efficiency and effectiveness of the company's operations.

Impact on Business Efficiency

By customizing Business Central to fit the organization's needs better, developers play a vital role in improving business processes. They enable companies to leverage the full potential of Business Central, ensuring the system supports specific workflows and provides valuable insights. This customization leads to more efficient operations, better decision-making, and ultimately a more competitive business.

Responsibilities of a Business Central Developer

Designing and Architecting Solutions

One of the primary responsibilities of a Business Central developer is to design and architect solutions that meet the specific needs of their organization. This involves understanding the business processes and requirements and then translating them into technical specifications. Developers must ensure that their designs are scalable and maintainable and integrate seamlessly with existing systems.

CHAPTER 1   INTRODUCTION TO DYNAMICS 365 BUSINESS CENTRAL DEVELOPMENT

Coding and Implementation

Once the design is in place, developers move on to coding and implementation. Using AL (Application Language), they write the necessary code to create extensions, customizations, and new features for Business Central. This phase requires a deep understanding of the AL Language and the Business Central framework. Developers must follow best practices to write clean, efficient, reliable, and reusable code.

Quality Assurance and Debugging

Testing is a crucial step in the development process. Business Central developers must thoroughly test their customizations to ensure they function correctly and do not introduce any new issues. This includes unit testing, integration testing, and user acceptance testing. Debugging is an integral part of this process, as developers need to identify and fix any bugs that arise during testing.

Tip   The latest update to Business Central includes enhanced debugging tools, making it easier than ever for developers to troubleshoot and optimize their code!

Deployment and Maintenance

After successful testing, developers deploy their solutions to the production environment. This step must be carefully managed to minimize disruption to business operations. Post deployment, developers are responsible for maintaining the solutions they have implemented. This includes monitoring performance, applying updates, and making necessary adjustments to ensure continued functionality and efficiency.

Collaboration and Communication

Effective communication and collaboration are essential for a Business Central developer. They must work closely with various stakeholders, including business analysts, functional consultants, project managers, and end users, to ensure that the solutions they develop meet business needs. This involves regular meetings, progress updates, and feedback sessions to keep everyone aligned and informed.

Certification Learning and Improvement

The field of technology is constantly evolving, and Business Central developers must stay updated with the latest trends, tools, and best practices. This includes ongoing education and training, attending workshops and conferences, and participating in online communities. Continuous learning ensures that developers can leverage new technologies and methodologies to improve their solutions and stay competitive in the industry.

Certification: To formalize and validate their expertise, developers should consider pursuing relevant certifications. The MB-820 certification, introduced this year, is specifically designed for Business Central developers. This certification assesses their ability to implement and manage Business Central solutions, enhancing their credentials and career prospects. For more details and to prepare for the MB-820 certification, visit the `https://learn.microsoft.com/en-us/credentials/certifications/d365-business-central-developer-associate/?practice-assessment-type=certification`.

Scenario: Upgrading an Existing Business Central System

Consider a scenario where a company needs to upgrade its existing Business Central system to the latest version to take advantage of new features and improvements. The Business Central developer would be responsible for

1. **Assessment and Planning**: Evaluating the current system, identifying customizations and extensions that need to be updated, and planning the upgrade process

2. **Code Refactoring and Updates**: Modifying existing code to ensure compatibility with the new version, including refactoring outdated code and implementing new features

3. **Testing**: Conducting extensive testing to ensure that the upgraded system functions correctly and that all customizations work as expected

4. **Deployment**: Carefully deploying the updated system to minimize downtime and ensure a smooth transition for end users

5. **Support and Maintenance**: Providing ongoing support to address any issues that arise post upgrade and making necessary adjustments to maintain system performance

In this scenario, the developer's role is critical in ensuring a successful upgrade, demonstrating the breadth and depth of responsibilities they handle.

CHAPTER 1   INTRODUCTION TO DYNAMICS 365 BUSINESS CENTRAL DEVELOPMENT

Checklist for the Roles and Responsibilities of a Business Central Developer

The role of a Dynamics 365 Business Central developer is multifaceted, involving a wide range of tasks and responsibilities that ensure the successful customization and implementation of Business Central solutions. This checklist serves as a comprehensive guide to the core duties and expectations for developers in this field. By following this checklist, developers can stay organized, maintain high standards of work, and ensure they are meeting the needs of their organization effectively. Whether you are new to Business Central development or an experienced professional, this checklist will help you cover all essential aspects of your role, from designing and coding to testing, deployment, and continuous improvement.

Designing and Architecting Solutions

- Understand business processes and requirements
- Translate business needs into technical specifications
- Ensure designs are scalable and maintainable and integrate with existing systems

Coding and Implementation

- Write clean, efficient, and reusable code using AL (Application Language)
- Follow best practices for coding standards
- Develop extensions, customizations, and new features for Business Central

Testing and Debugging

- Conduct unit testing to validate individual components
- Perform integration testing to ensure components work together
- Engage in user acceptance testing to confirm solutions meet user needs
- Identify and fix bugs during testing

Deployment and Maintenance

- Plan and manage the deployment process to minimize business disruption
- Monitor system performance post deployment
- Apply updates and make necessary adjustments to maintain functionality

Collaboration and Communication

- Work closely with business analysts, project managers, and end users
- Participate in regular meetings and provide progress updates
- Gather feedback and make adjustments based on stakeholder input

Continuous Learning and Improvement

- Stay updated with the latest trends, tools, and best practices in Business Central development
- Attend workshops, conferences, and training sessions
- Participate in online communities and forums

Additional Responsibilities

- Conduct regular code reviews to maintain code quality
- Document all customizations and solutions for future reference
- Provide training and support to end users and other developers

Introduction to AL Language and Its Significance

Why AL Language?

AL (Application Language) is specifically designed for developing solutions within Dynamics 365 Business Central. The primary reason for using AL is its deep integration with the Business Central environment. AL allows developers to extend and customize the platform efficiently, ensuring that all customizations work seamlessly with the core application without disrupting its stability and performance.

CHAPTER 1　INTRODUCTION TO DYNAMICS 365 BUSINESS CENTRAL DEVELOPMENT

Uniqueness of AL Language

The uniqueness of AL lies in its targeted functionality and integration capabilities. Unlike general-purpose programming languages, AL is optimized for business application development within Business Central. This specialization allows developers to focus on creating business logic and workflows tailored to their organization's needs. AL is built to handle the specific requirements of enterprise resource planning (ERP) systems, such as handling financial transactions, inventory management, and supply chain operations.

Comparison with Other Languages

The table below compares AL programming with other programming languages such as Python, .NET, and JavaScript.

Feature/aspect	AL	Python	.NET (C#)	JavaScript
Purpose	ERP customization in Business Central	General-purpose: web development, data analysis, AI	General-purpose: web, desktop, mobile, cloud applications	Web development and interactive front-end applications
Syntax	Business-centric, optimized for ERP tasks	Simple, versatile, easy to read and write	Complex, supports multiple paradigms	Scripting for dynamic web content
Integration	Natively integrated with Business Central	Requires libraries/frameworks for ERP integration	Integrates with ERP via APIs and SDKs	Interacts with ERP through web services and APIs

(*continued*)

Table 1-1. (*continued*)

Feature/ aspect	AL	Python	.NET (C#)	JavaScript
Use case	Customizing and extending Business Central functionalities	Data science, automation, web apps, AI development	Enterprise applications, broad development scope beyond ERP	Enhancing web interfaces, creating dynamic content

Overview of Development Tools and Environments

Introduction to Development Tools

Developing solutions for Dynamics 365 Business Central requires a suite of specialized tools that facilitate coding, testing, and deploying customizations. The primary development tool used by Business Central developers is Visual Studio Code (VS Code), a versatile and powerful code editor that supports AL Language development through the AL Language extension.

Visual Studio Code

Visual Studio Code (VS Code) is the recommended IDE for developing AL code. It offers numerous features that streamline the development process:

- **AL Language Extension**: This extension provides syntax highlighting, IntelliSense, debugging capabilities, and snippets specifically for AL development.

- **Source Control Integration**: VS Code integrates with Git, enabling version control and collaboration on code projects.

- **Customization and Extensions**: Developers can install various extensions to enhance their productivity, such as tools for better code management, testing, and deployment.

Tip Visual Studio Code now supports even more extensions tailored specifically for AL development, boosting productivity and collaboration!

Business Central Sandbox Environment

A sandbox environment is essential for development and testing purposes. It provides a safe space to create, test, and validate customizations without affecting the live production environment:

- **Creating a Sandbox**: Business Central allows developers to create multiple sandbox environments. These environments replicate the production setup and include all necessary data for realistic testing.

- **Testing Customizations**: Sandboxes enable thorough testing of customizations and extensions, ensuring they work correctly before being deployed to the live system.

Source Control Systems

Source control systems like Git are crucial for managing changes to the codebase. They allow multiple developers to collaborate on the same project, track changes, and manage versions effectively.

- **Version Control**: Using Git, developers can track changes, revert to previous versions, and manage branches for different features or releases.

- **Collaboration**: Source control facilitates collaboration by allowing multiple developers to work on the same codebase simultaneously, resolving conflicts, and merging changes.

Deployment Tools

Deploying customizations and extensions to Business Central involves several steps, for which specialized tools and processes are used:

- **Extension Management**: Business Central uses extensions to manage customizations. Developers package their AL code into extensions, which can be deployed to the environment.

- **AppSource**: For distributing customizations publicly, developers can submit their extensions to Microsoft AppSource. This marketplace allows other Business Central users to discover and install extensions.

Scenario: Developing and Deploying a Custom Module

Consider a scenario where a developer needs to create a custom quality assurance, import costing module for a client. The process involves several steps:

1. **Development in VS Code**: The developer writes the AL code for the module using VS Code, leveraging the AL Language extension for enhanced productivity.

2. **Testing in Sandbox**: The custom module is tested extensively in a sandbox environment to ensure it meets the client's requirements and functions correctly without affecting the existing system.

3. **Version Control with Git**: Throughout the development process, the developer uses Git to manage changes, collaborate with team members, and maintain a history of the project.

4. **Deployment**: Once tested and approved, the custom module is packaged as an extension and deployed to the client's production environment, ensuring a smooth transition and minimal disruption to operations.

Conclusion

In this chapter, we've explored the dynamic world of Dynamics 365 Business Central development, delving into its key roles, responsibilities, and the significance of the AL Language. We've examined how Business

CHAPTER 1   INTRODUCTION TO DYNAMICS 365 BUSINESS CENTRAL DEVELOPMENT

Central addresses common business challenges with its unified platform, automation capabilities, and real-time data access, enhancing overall efficiency and decision-making.

Understanding the role of a Business Central developer and mastering tools like Visual Studio Code and sandbox environments are crucial for leveraging the full potential of Business Central. With its continuous evolution, from advanced development tools to innovative features, Business Central stands out as a powerful solution for modern businesses.

Key Takeaways

1. **Understanding the Development Role**
   - A Business Central developer plays a crucial role in customizing and enhancing the Dynamics 365 Business Central platform to meet specific business needs. This includes designing, coding, testing, and deploying solutions.

2. **Core Responsibilities**
   - Key responsibilities include creating technical specifications, writing and maintaining AL code, testing customizations, managing deployments, and collaborating with stakeholders.

3. **Significance of AL Language**
   - AL is the programming language used for Business Central development. Its unique integration with the platform allows for effective customization and management of ERP processes, differing significantly from general-purpose languages like Python or .NET.

4. **Development Tools and Environments**
   - Tools such as Visual Studio Code and sandbox environments are essential for effective development and testing. These tools provide a robust framework for managing customizations and ensuring code quality.

5. **Key Benefits of Business Central**
   - Business Central improves efficiency by automating processes and centralizing data. It enhances decision-making through real-time insights and reporting and offers scalability to support business growth.

6. **Real-World Impact**
   - Implementing Business Central can lead to significant operational improvements, including increased efficiency, better data accuracy, and enhanced decision-making capabilities. Real-world examples highlight how businesses have transformed their operations with Business Central.

7. **Ongoing Learning and Adaptation**
   - The field of Business Central development is continuously evolving with new features and tools. Staying updated with these advancements and embracing new technologies is crucial for maximizing the benefits of the platform and maintaining a competitive edge.

CHAPTER 1　INTRODUCTION TO DYNAMICS 365 BUSINESS CENTRAL DEVELOPMENT

Exercise

Analyzing the Benefits of Business Central

Objective: Evaluate the benefits of using Dynamics 365 Business Central in a real-world scenario.

1. **Task**: Read a case study about a company that implemented Business Central.

2. **Instructions**

    - Identify the key challenges the company faced before implementing Business Central.

    - Analyze how Business Central helped address these challenges.

    - Summarize the benefits the company experienced post implementation.

3. **Questions**

    - What were the primary challenges addressed by Business Central?

    - How did Business Central improve the company's efficiency and decision-making?

Exercise Solution: Analyzing the Benefits of Business Central

Case Study Summary: A mid-sized manufacturing company, XYZ Manufacturing, implemented Dynamics 365 Business Central to streamline its operations. Prior to the implementation, the company faced several challenges that hindered its growth and efficiency.

Key Challenges Faced by XYZ Manufacturing Before Implementing Business Central

1. **Fragmented Systems**
   - XYZ Manufacturing used multiple disparate systems for managing finance, inventory, sales, and customer service. This fragmentation led to data silos, making it difficult to get a unified view of the business.

2. **Manual Processes**
   - Many business processes were manual, including order processing, invoicing, and inventory management. This not only slowed down operations but also increased the risk of human error.

3. **Inconsistent Data**
   - Due to the use of multiple systems, data consistency was a major issue. Different departments had their own versions of data, leading to discrepancies and miscommunication.

4. **Lack of Real-Time Insights**
   - The company struggled with decision-making because of a lack of real-time data. Reports were generated manually, which delayed access to critical business insights.

How Business Central Helped Address These Challenges

1. **Unified Platform**
   - Business Central replaced the fragmented systems with a single, unified platform. This integration eliminated data silos and provided a comprehensive view of all business operations.

2. **Automation of Processes**
   - The platform automated key business processes, such as order processing, invoicing, and inventory management. This automation reduced manual effort and minimized errors.

3. **Data Consistency**
   - With all data centralized in Business Central, data consistency improved significantly. The company now had a single source of truth, which enhanced accuracy and reliability of information across departments.

4. **Real-Time Data Access**
   - Business Central provided real-time access to data, enabling the company to generate instant reports and gain insights quickly. This real-time data availability improved the decision-making process, allowing for more timely and informed decisions.

Benefits Experienced by XYZ Manufacturing Post Implementation

1. **Increased Efficiency**

    - Automation of manual processes and a unified platform led to a significant increase in operational efficiency. The company reported a 30% reduction in order processing time and a 20% improvement in overall productivity.

2. **Enhanced Decision-Making**

    - Real-time access to data and advanced reporting tools allowed managers to make more informed decisions. This improved forecasting accuracy and enabled the company to respond swiftly to market changes.

3. **Improved Data Accuracy**

    - With consistent and centralized data, the company experienced fewer errors and discrepancies. This reliability of data improved internal communication and coordination among departments.

4. **Scalability and Flexibility**

    - The modular design of Business Central allowed XYZ Manufacturing to easily scale its operations as the business grew. The company could add new functionalities and users without disrupting ongoing activities.

Answers to the Questions:

1. **What were the primary challenges addressed by Business Central?**

    - The primary challenges addressed by Business Central included fragmented systems, manual processes, inconsistent data, and lack of real-time insights.

2. **How did Business Central improve the company's efficiency and decision-making?**

    - Business Central improved the company's efficiency by automating manual processes and providing a unified platform for all business operations. It enhanced decision-making by offering real-time access to data and advanced reporting tools, which enabled timely and informed decisions. The consistency and reliability of data further contributed to better internal communication and coordination.

CHAPTER 2

Installation, Development, and Deployment for Business Central Chapter

This chapter provides a comprehensive guide to the essential processes involved in working with Dynamics 365 Business Central, focusing specifically on the sandbox environment. It begins with clear, step-by-step instructions on the installation procedures within the sandbox, ensuring a smooth setup for testing and development. Following this, the chapter delves into the development process, covering the design, development, and testing of solutions to meet business needs effectively within the sandbox. Deployment strategies for Business Central apps in a sandbox environment are then explored, offering practical approaches to roll out applications seamlessly. Finally, the chapter addresses integrating with Microsoft Power Platform products, showcasing how to enhance Business Central's capabilities through powerful integrations.

CHAPTER 2   INSTALLATION, DEVELOPMENT, AND DEPLOYMENT FOR BUSINESS
            CENTRAL CHAPTER

Throughout the chapter, various tips are provided to enhance the working experience with the sandbox environment, ensuring readers can navigate and utilize its features effectively. Additionally, exercises are included to reinforce the learning and practical application of the concepts discussed. These exercises will guide readers through real-world scenarios, from setting up their sandbox environment to deploying and integrating solutions, ensuring a hands-on understanding of the processes.

By the end of this chapter, readers will have a solid understanding of how to install Business Central in a sandbox, develop tailored solutions, deploy applications efficiently in a sandbox environment, and integrate with the Microsoft Power Platform. This foundational knowledge will empower readers to effectively manage and optimize their Business Central sandbox environment, preparing them for more advanced topics and real-world applications.

Managing Sandbox Environments

Managing sandbox environments effectively is crucial for maintaining a robust development and testing workflow in Business Central. By default, provisioning Business Central includes one production and three sandbox environments. It's advisable to name these sandboxes strategically, such as Dev, UAT, and GOLD. The GOLD environment should hold the latest backup from production, serving as a stable reference point for significant fixes. The Dev environment can be used for active development work, while UAT (user acceptance testing) ensures that all changes meet business requirements before moving to production. This structured approach ensures that development, testing, and deployment are handled in an organized manner, reducing risks and enhancing the quality of the final product.

AppSource Submission

Publishing an app to Microsoft AppSource is an intricate process that involves becoming a registered ISV (independent software vendor) partner with Microsoft. This partnership grants access to an exclusive object ID range necessary for app development. However, AppSource submissions are not just about coding—Microsoft enforces stringent standards for coding practices, documentation, and testing rigor. The process includes adhering to a predefined naming convention, thorough testing, and comprehensive documentation to ensure the app meets the high standards required for public distribution. Due to its complexity, AppSource submission could warrant an entire chapter of its own, and while it's an option for developers, it may extend beyond the scope of this book.

Prerequisites

Before starting, ensure you have

1. A work or school account
2. An activated trial version from Dynamics 365 Business Central
3. Visual Studio Code installed
4. The AL Language extension for Microsoft Dynamics 365 Business Central

CHAPTER 2 INSTALLATION, DEVELOPMENT, AND DEPLOYMENT FOR BUSINESS CENTRAL CHAPTER

Getting Started with Visual Studio Code for Business Central Development

Microsoft uses Visual Studio Code as the primary development environment for Dynamics 365 Business Central. Visual Studio Code, launched in April 2015, is a free, open-source code editor distinct from Visual Studio, which is geared toward creating, building, and deploying large .NET solutions.

Installation

Visual Studio Code can be installed on Windows, Linux, and macOS. You can download and install it from the Visual Studio Code website.

Features of Visual Studio Code

With Visual Studio Code, you can write Application Language (AL) code to create extensions for Microsoft Dynamics 365 Business Central. AL is the language used to create and access objects, write business logic, and develop custom functionalities.

Extensions in Visual Studio Code

Visual Studio Code supports the concept of extensions, which are small packages designed to extend the standard functionality of the solution. By default, Visual Studio Code supports several basic programming and markup languages such as HTML, JavaScript, and CSS. To develop Business Central solutions, you need to install the AL Language extension provided by Microsoft.

CHAPTER 2 INSTALLATION, DEVELOPMENT, AND DEPLOYMENT FOR BUSINESS CENTRAL CHAPTER

Getting Started with Visual Studio Code

After launching Visual Studio Code, you will see the Welcome page, which provides links to start creating new projects, open recent folders, or access help resources.

Key Components of the Visual Studio Code Interface:

- **Activity Bar**: Located on the left side of the Welcome page, the Activity Bar contains several essential tabs:
- **Explorer Tab**: Shows the active folder with the files you're working on
- **Search Tab**: Allows searching and replacing text values within files, with options to include or exclude specific files
- **Source Control Tab**: Manages source control systems, with built-in support for Git and options to install other extensions like Visual Studio Team Foundation
- **Run (Debug) Tab**: Enables you to step through your code for debugging purposes
- **Extensions Tab**: Where you can install and manage Visual Studio Code extensions, including the AL Language extension for Business Central development

Using AL Language in Visual Studio Code

To start developing Business Central solutions, install the AL Language extension. This extension enables you to

CHAPTER 2 INSTALLATION, DEVELOPMENT, AND DEPLOYMENT FOR BUSINESS CENTRAL CHAPTER

- Create AL projects
- Develop and test extensions
- Access Business Central objects and write custom business logic

Installing the AL Language Extension in Visual Studio Code

When developing applications for Microsoft Dynamics 365 Business Central using Visual Studio Code, it is essential to install the AL Language extension. This extension provides the necessary tools to write AL code, which is used for creating and accessing objects and writing business logic in Business Central.

Installation Steps

1. **Open Visual Studio Code**
   - Launch Visual Studio Code on your system.

2. **Access Extensions**
   - Select the Extensions tab from the Activity Bar on the left side of the Visual Studio Code application.
   - Alternatively, you can use the Ctrl + Shift + X keyboard shortcut to open the Extensions view.

3. **Search for AL Language**
   - In the Search Extensions in Marketplace field, type "AL Language".

4. **Install the Extension**

    - Click on the green Install button next to the AL Language extension to install it.

Post Installation

After the installation, the AL Language extension is activated. You are now ready to start developing extensions for Business Central. To keep your development environment up-to-date, Microsoft provides frequent updates to the AL Language extension, often linked to the latest versions of Business Central.

Testing and Debugging Your Application

Microsoft provides three primary methods to test and debug your Business Central applications:

1. **Online Cloud Sandbox**

    - Use the online cloud sandbox environment to test and debug your extensions.

2. **Docker Images**

    - Docker images are particularly useful when multiple developers are concurrently working on building extensions. They allow you to replicate the versions deployed in the cloud sandbox or on-premises environments.

    - Developers can use these Docker images to test extensions on various versions, including upcoming or beta releases available through the Microsoft Collaborate program.

- Additionally, Docker supports "Test Code," which can automate some aspects of development testing, streamlining the testing process.

3. **On-Premise Version**

   - Test and debug your application using the on-premise version of Business Central.

Using Docker Images for Upcoming Releases

When working with Docker images of upcoming releases, follow these steps to use the updated AL Language extension:

1. **Disable the Marketplace Extension**

   - Select the AL Language extension in Visual Studio Code and click on the Disable button.

2. **Install from VSIX File**

   - Click on the ellipsis (...) above the Search Extensions in Marketplace field.
   - Select "Install from VSIX..." from the menu.
   - Browse to your downloaded VSIX file and install the extension.

Managing Prerelease Versions

To install and manage prerelease versions of the AL Language extension:

1. **Install Prerelease Version**

   - Use the drop-down list in the Visual Studio Code extension management page for the AL Language extension to select "Install Pre-Release Version".

2. **Switch Between Versions**

- If the prerelease version is already installed, use the "Switch to Pre-Release Version" option.

- The extension management page will indicate if a prerelease version is being used and provide an option to switch back to the release version.

Actual Steps for Installation and Configuration

1. Sign Up for a Dynamics 365 Business Central Sandbox

- Visit the `https://signup.microsoft.com` and create your sandbox environment.

2. Download and Install Visual Studio Code

- Download Visual Studio Code from the `https://code.visualstudio.com` and install it on your machine as shown in Figure 2-1.

CHAPTER 2   INSTALLATION, DEVELOPMENT, AND DEPLOYMENT FOR BUSINESS
            CENTRAL CHAPTER

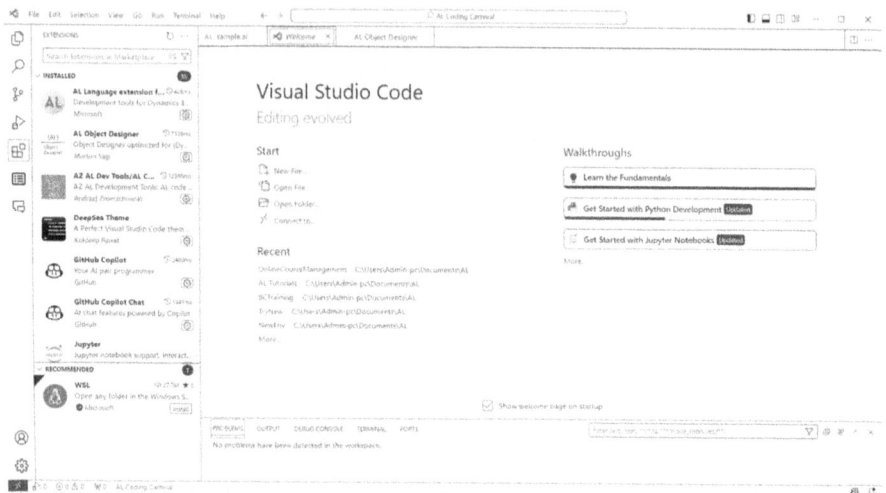

Figure 2-1. *Visual Studio Code Interface*

3. Install the AL Language Extension

- Open Visual Studio Code, go to the Extensions view, and search for "AL Language." Install the extension provided by Microsoft as shown in Figure 2-2.

CHAPTER 2   INSTALLATION, DEVELOPMENT, AND DEPLOYMENT FOR BUSINESS
             CENTRAL CHAPTER

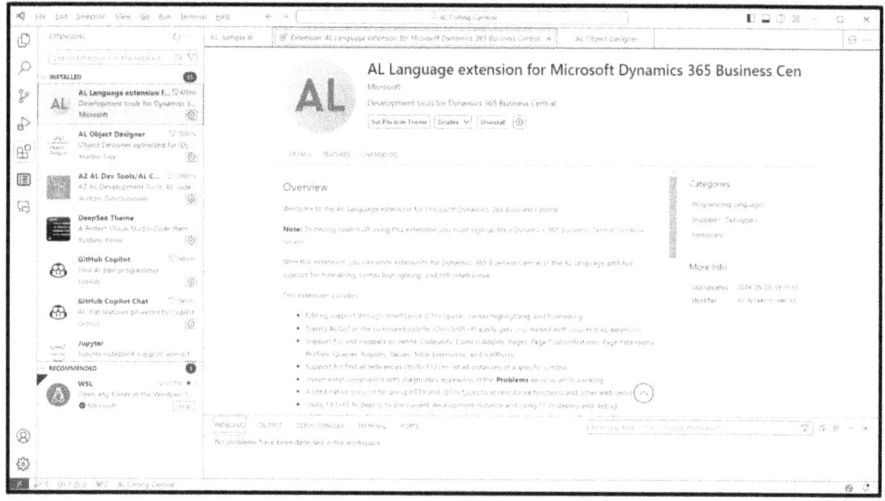

Figure 2-2. *AL Language Extension*

4. Set Up Your Development Environment

- Press Ctrl + Shift + P to open the Command Palette.

- Select AL: Go! (as shown in Figure 2-3) to create a new project. Choose a new folder for your project and select the Microsoft Cloud sandbox as the server.

- Follow the steps in Figures 2-3 to 2-11.

CHAPTER 2 INSTALLATION, DEVELOPMENT, AND DEPLOYMENT FOR BUSINESS
         CENTRAL CHAPTER

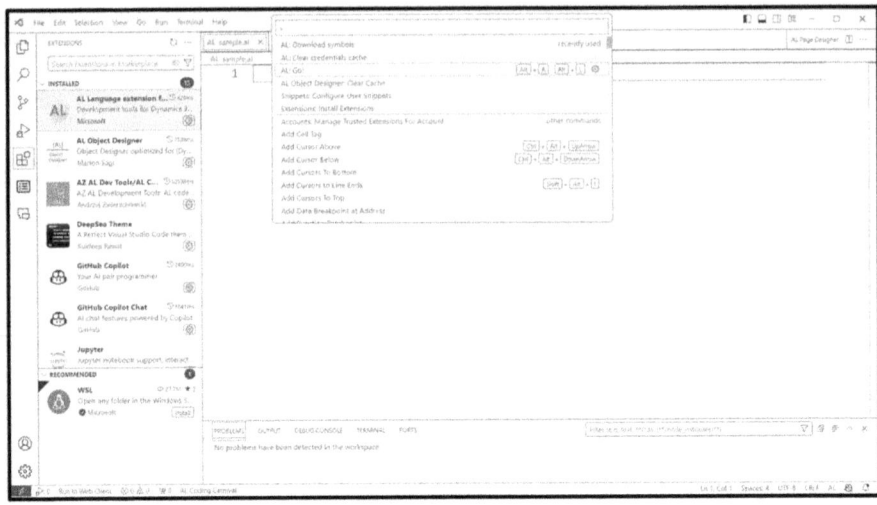

Figure 2-3. *AL:Go*

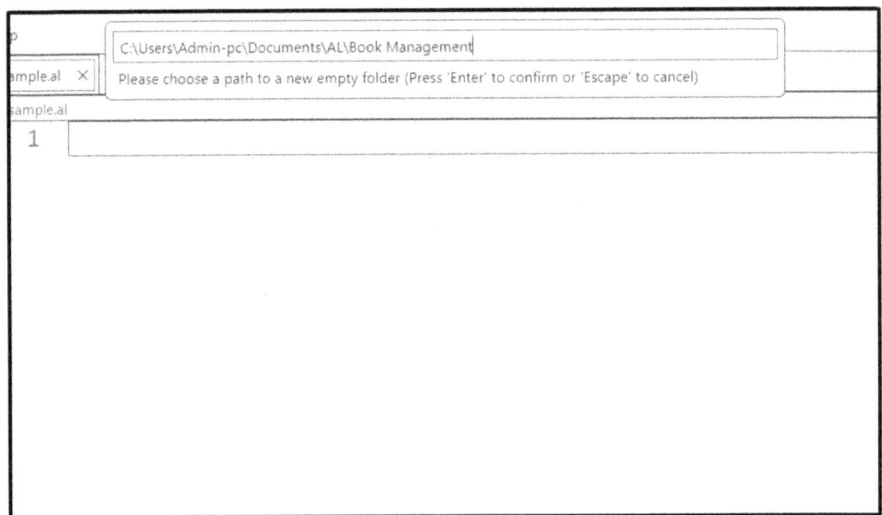

Figure 2-4. *Give Your Extension a Name*

CHAPTER 2 INSTALLATION, DEVELOPMENT, AND DEPLOYMENT FOR BUSINESS CENTRAL CHAPTER

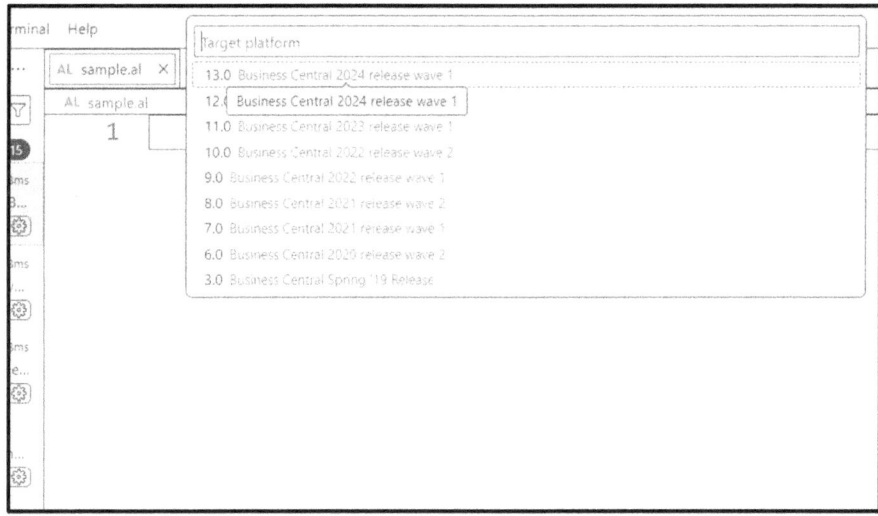

Figure 2-5. *Select the Business Central Version*

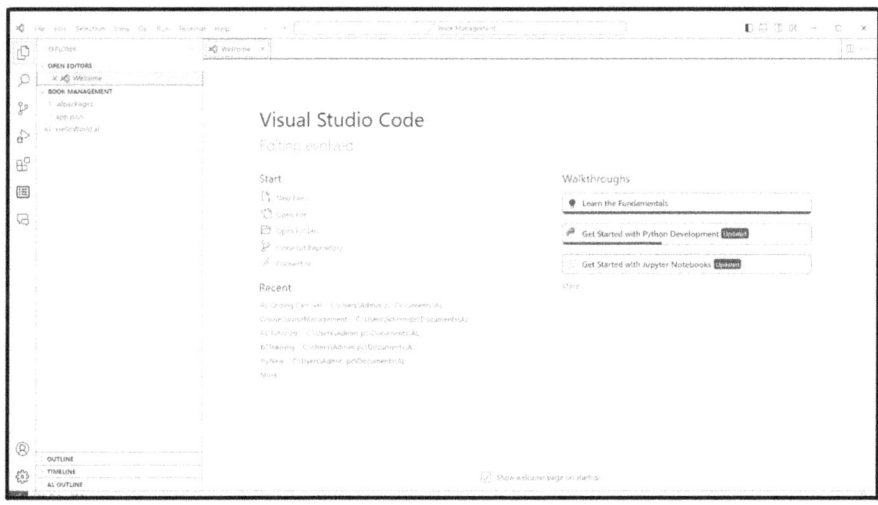

Figure 2-6. *Your Extension Is Created*

CHAPTER 2　INSTALLATION, DEVELOPMENT, AND DEPLOYMENT FOR BUSINESS CENTRAL CHAPTER

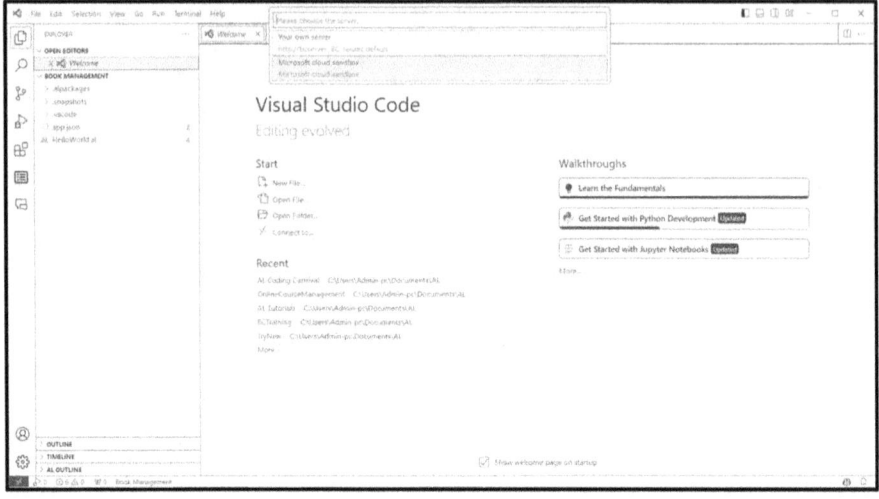

Figure 2-7. *Select Your Option (Cloud Sandbox in Our Scenario)*

5. Configure Your Project

Update the `launch.json` file with the following settings:

```
{
  "server": "https://your-sandbox-url",
  "serverInstance": "BC",
  "authentication": "UserPassword"
}
```

- Replace `"https://your-sandbox-url"` with the URL of your sandbox environment.

CHAPTER 2 INSTALLATION, DEVELOPMENT, AND DEPLOYMENT FOR BUSINESS CENTRAL CHAPTER

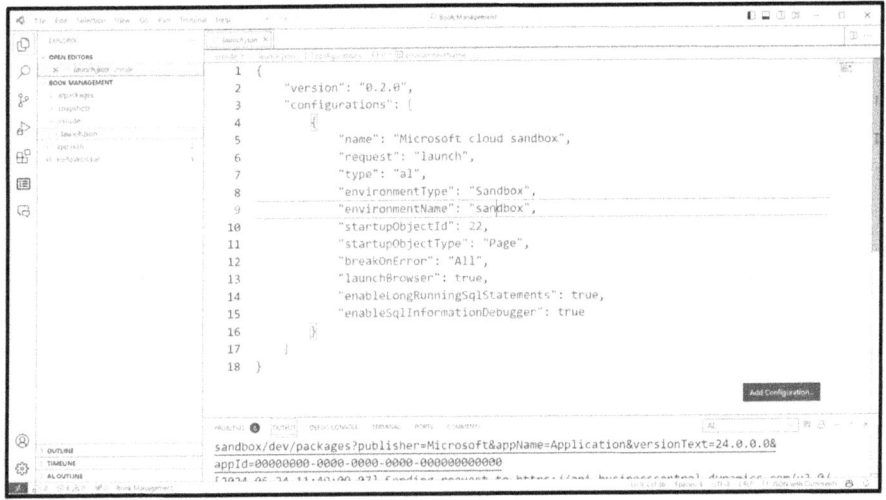

Figure 2-8. *Ensure the launc.json Is Properly Configured*

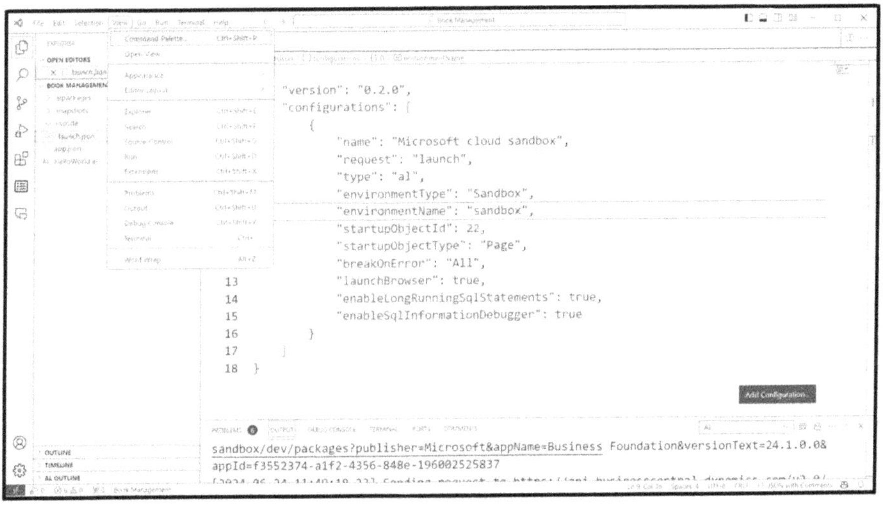

Figure 2-9. *Next Step Is Download the Symbols*

CHAPTER 2   INSTALLATION, DEVELOPMENT, AND DEPLOYMENT FOR BUSINESS
            CENTRAL CHAPTER

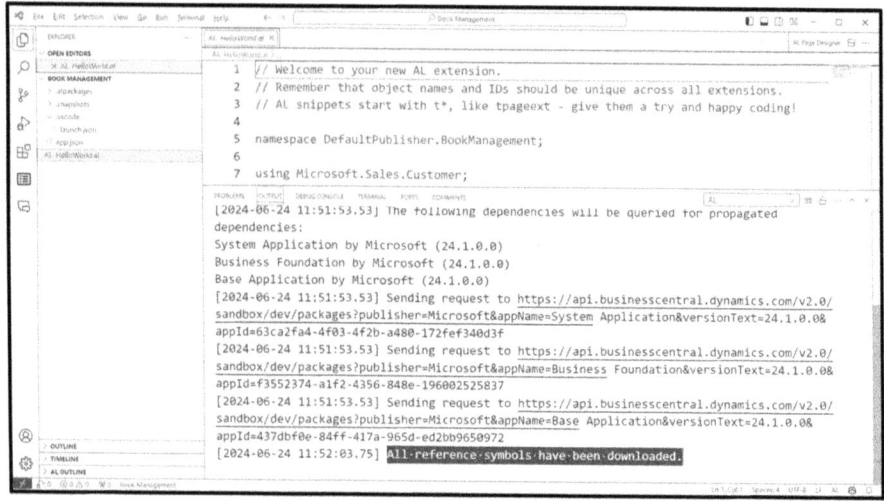

Figure 2-10. AL: Download Symbols

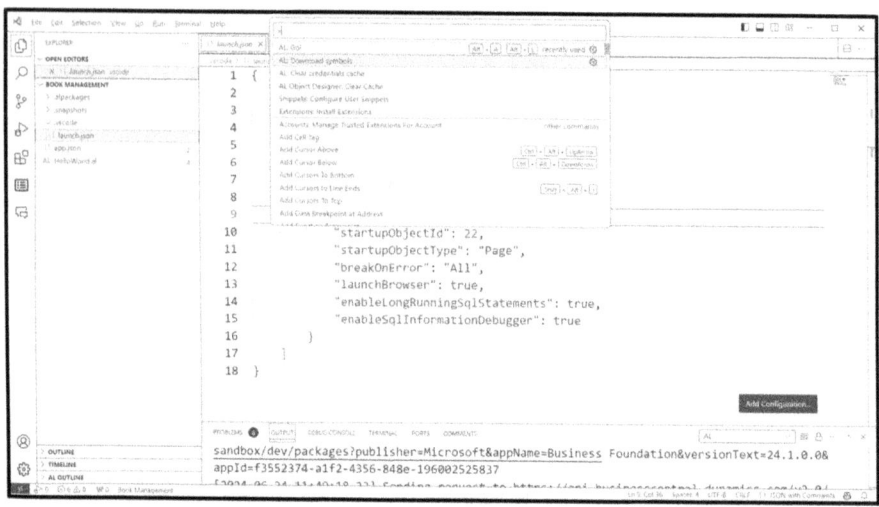

Figure 2-11. You Should See This Message "All reference symbols have been downloaded"

6. Deploy and Run Your Extension

- Press Ctrl + F5 to deploy and run your extension on the online sandbox tenant. If Ctrl + F5 does not work, select "Run Without Debugging" from the Run menu.

Tips for Enhancing Your Development Experience

- Use Ctrl + Space to activate IntelliSense, which helps in code completion.

- Utilize built-in snippets by typing t and selecting from the list.

- Create objects within the appropriate object ranges to avoid conflicts.

- Refer to sample projects available on GitHub.

Discovering the Logical Database and Its Objects

Dynamics 365 Business Central is a cloud-based application built on top of a robust database. This database houses not only the data, such as customer, vendor, and product information, but also every object used within the application. This architecture allows developers to quickly add, modify, and deploy new solutions without the need to rebuild the entire product.

Core Object Types

Table: Defines how data is stored and retrieved. Each table contains fields that correspond to data attributes.

Page: Provides the interface for users to view, add, modify, or delete records in a table. Pages define the layout and structure of the data presentation.

Report: Used for printing, processing, or previewing data in specific layouts. Reports enable the formatted output of data for business use.

Codeunit: A container for AL code, allowing for the grouping of reusable functions that can be called from other objects.

Query: Provides a relational data model for efficient querying of the database, enabling the retrieval of specific datasets.

XMLPort: Facilitates the import and export of data in XML or text formats, useful for data exchange with external systems.

Extending Business Central

Business Central includes built-in functionality through its objects, which can be extended but not directly modified. This extensibility allows for customization while maintaining the integrity of the core application.

Table Extension: Extends the functionality of existing tables by adding new fields or modifying existing ones.

Page Extension: Enhances existing pages by adding new controls or modifying the layout.

Logical Database Structure

In Business Central, data is organized into different companies, with each company's data stored as records in various tables. These tables consist of multiple fields representing different data attributes. While data is company specific, objects created by developers are applicable across all companies within the same database.

Object Numbering Conventions

Each object in Business Central is identified by a unique number. This numbering system helps in organizing version management, localization, and customization and ensures successful upgrades:

- **0-49,999**: Objects used by Microsoft for worldwide versions

- **100,000-999,999**: Localized objects designed for specific countries and regions, also created by Microsoft

- **50,000-99,999**: Reserved for tenant/customization by partners

- **1,000,000-60,000,000**: Registered Solution Program (RSP) for ISV solutions, available in both on-premises and cloud versions of Business Central

- **70,000,000-74,999,999**: Reserved for extension development and typically available as apps from AppSource

Managing Objects

Before creating new objects, it's important to follow object numbering conventions to maintain organization and ensure compatibility with future updates. Using prefixes or suffixes helps avoid naming conflicts, especially when multiple extensions are installed. A prefix or suffix should be a unique tag of at least three characters registered with Microsoft.

General Rules

- Prefix/suffix must be at least three characters.
- Object/field names must start or end with the prefix/suffix.
- In case of conflicts, the registered prefix/suffix takes precedence.
- Use the AppSourceCop tool to check for missing prefixes/suffixes and ensure compliance.

Development Process: Designing, Developing, and Testing Solutions

Designing Solutions

Designing a solution in Dynamics 365 Business Central involves understanding business requirements and translating them into a structured plan. This process starts with requirements gathering, where the needs and challenges of the business are documented. The next step is to create a high-level design that outlines how the solution will meet these requirements. This design includes defining the data model, business logic, user interface, and integration points with other systems. Effective design ensures that the solution is scalable and maintainable and aligns with best practices.

Developing Solutions

Development in Business Central is primarily done using AL (Application Language) in Visual Studio Code. The development process includes

1. **Setting Up the Development Environment**: This involves installing Visual Studio Code and the AL Language extension and setting up a sandbox environment for development and testing.

2. **Creating Extensions**: Developers create extensions by defining new AL objects like tables, pages, codeunits, and reports. These extensions encapsulate the customizations and new features added to Business Central.

3. **Writing Code**: Developers write AL code to implement the business logic. This includes creating procedures, handling events, and using built-in AL functions and libraries to manipulate data and interact with the system.

4. **Debugging**: Visual Studio Code provides debugging tools to step through the code, inspect variables, and diagnose issues. Developers use breakpoints, watch expressions, and other debugging features to ensure the code behaves as expected.

CHAPTER 2   INSTALLATION, DEVELOPMENT, AND DEPLOYMENT FOR BUSINESS
            CENTRAL CHAPTER

Testing Solutions

Testing is a critical phase in the development process to ensure the solution is robust and meets the business requirements. The testing process includes

1. **Unit Testing**: Developers write unit tests to validate individual pieces of code. This involves creating test codeunits that test the functionality of specific AL procedures or functions.

2. **Integration Testing**: This testing phase ensures that the new extensions integrate seamlessly with existing Business Central functionality and other systems. It involves testing data flow, user interactions, and business processes end to end.

3. **User Acceptance Testing (UAT)**: The solution is deployed to a test environment where end users perform UAT. This phase verifies that the solution meets the business requirements and is ready for production use. Feedback from UAT is used to make any necessary adjustments.

Deployment

After thorough testing, the solution is deployed to the production environment. Deployment involves packaging the extensions, publishing them to the Business Central environment, and configuring any necessary settings. Postdeployment activities include monitoring the system, providing user training, and supporting the solution to address any issues that arise.

Tips for Enhancing Development and Testing

- **Use Version Control**: Implement version control using Git to track changes, collaborate with team members, and manage different versions of the code.

- **Automate Testing**: Use automated testing tools to streamline the testing process and ensure consistent quality.

- **Documentation**: Maintain thorough documentation of the design, development, and testing processes to facilitate knowledge transfer and future maintenance.

Deployment Strategies for Business Central Apps

Deploying applications in Dynamics 365 Business Central involves several strategic steps to ensure a smooth and efficient rollout of new functionalities and customizations. This section covers the key deployment strategies for Business Central apps, focusing on best practices and essential considerations for a successful deployment process.

1. Preparing for Deployment

Before deploying any Business Central app, thorough preparation is crucial. This includes

- **Testing in a Sandbox Environment**: Ensure that the app has been thoroughly tested in a sandbox environment to identify and resolve any issues. This step helps simulate the production environment and catch potential bugs before the app goes live.

CHAPTER 2   INSTALLATION, DEVELOPMENT, AND DEPLOYMENT FOR BUSINESS CENTRAL CHAPTER

- **Backup of Existing Data**: Create a backup of the current production environment. This safeguard ensures that you can restore the system to its previous state if any issues arise during deployment.

- **Documentation**: Maintain detailed documentation of the app's functionality, installation steps, and configuration settings. This documentation will be valuable during the deployment process and for future maintenance.

2. Using AL Extensions

Business Central apps are developed as AL extensions, which are packages containing the customizations and new features. The deployment process involves publishing these extensions to the Business Central environment.

- **Creating the Extension Package**: Package the app's components (tables, pages, codeunits, etc.) into an extension file (.app). Ensure the package includes all necessary dependencies and meets the Business Central app standards.

- **Publishing the Extension**: Use Visual Studio Code or the Business Central Administration Shell to publish the extension to the target environment. The `Publish` command uploads the extension package to the Business Central server.

3. Managing Versions and Updates

Managing different versions of the app and deploying updates requires careful planning.

- **Version Control**: Use a version control system (e.g., Git) to manage changes and maintain different versions of the app. This approach helps track modifications and collaborate with other developers.

- **Incremental Updates**: Deploy updates incrementally to minimize disruptions. Test updates thoroughly in a sandbox environment before rolling them out to production.

- **AppSource for Public Apps**: Publishing a public app to Microsoft AppSource is an option for broader distribution. However, it is a complex process that involves additional steps. To publish an app to AppSource, you need to register as an ISV partner with Microsoft. This involves obtaining an exclusive object range, adhering to specific coding and documentation standards, and using a standard prefix. Microsoft has strict guidelines and certification processes for AppSource submissions.

Given the complexity and breadth of this topic, it may be beyond the scope of this book. For those interested, detailed information and guidance are available through Microsoft's official resources or experienced ISV partners.

4. Multitenant Deployments

For apps intended for multiple tenants, consider the following strategies:

- **Tenant Customization**: Ensure the app is customizable to meet the specific needs of different tenants. Use configuration settings and extension points to allow tenant-specific customizations.

- **Isolated Environments**: Deploy the app in isolated environments for each tenant to prevent cross-tenant data access and ensure data privacy.

5. Postdeployment Activities

After deploying the app, several postdeployment activities are essential to ensure smooth operation:

- **Monitoring and Support**: Monitor the app's performance and user feedback. Address any issues promptly and provide support to users as needed.

- **Training and Documentation**: Offer training sessions and provide comprehensive documentation to help users understand and utilize the new functionalities effectively.

- **Regular Maintenance**: Schedule regular maintenance and updates to keep the app up-to-date with the latest features and security patches.

6. Rollback Strategy

Have a rollback strategy in place in case of deployment failures. This involves

- **Backup Restoration**: Use the backups created before deployment to restore the system to its previous state.

- **Reverting Changes**: If issues are identified after deployment, revert the app to a stable version and address the problems before attempting another deployment.

Tips for Successful Deployment

- **Automation**: Automate repetitive tasks in the deployment process using scripts and tools to reduce errors and save time.

- **Continuous Integration/Continuous Deployment (CI/CD)**: Implement CI/CD pipelines to streamline the build, test, and deployment processes, ensuring faster and more reliable deployments. For example, Azure DevOps is a robust platform that can be used to create and manage CI/CD pipelines effectively. It offers tools for automating builds, tests, and deployments, enhancing the overall efficiency of the development lifecycle.

- **User Communication**: Keep users informed about deployment schedules, potential downtime, and new features. Clear communication helps manage user expectations and minimizes disruptions.

CHAPTER 2 INSTALLATION, DEVELOPMENT, AND DEPLOYMENT FOR BUSINESS CENTRAL CHAPTER

Deployment Strategies Checklist for Business Central Apps

Predeployment Preparation

- **Sandbox Testing**
  - Thoroughly test the app in a sandbox environment.
  - Verify all functionalities and integrations.
- **Data Backup**
  - Create a full backup of the current production environment.
  - Ensure backup integrity and accessibility.
- **Documentation**
  - Prepare detailed documentation for the app, including installation steps, configuration settings, and user guides.
- **Review Permissions and Licenses**
  - Verify that necessary permissions and licenses are in place for accessing required objects.

Deployment Process

- **Create Extension Package**
  - Package all components of the app (tables, pages, codeunits, etc.) into an AL extension file (.app).
  - Ensure all dependencies are included and properly configured.

CHAPTER 2   INSTALLATION, DEVELOPMENT, AND DEPLOYMENT FOR BUSINESS
            CENTRAL CHAPTER

- **Publish Extension**
  - Use Visual Studio Code or the Business Central Administration Shell to publish the extension.
  - Command: `Publish-BCContainerApp -containerName <containerName> -appFile <pathToAppFile> -tenant <tenantId>`
- **Version Management**
  - Maintain version control using systems like Git.
  - Document all changes and updates.
- **Incremental Updates**
  - Test updates incrementally in a sandbox environment.
  - Deploy updates incrementally to the production environment to minimize disruptions.
- **Public Apps via AppSource**
  - Follow Microsoft's guidelines for submitting apps to AppSource.
  - Ensure the app meets all certification requirements.

Multitenant Deployment

- **Customization**
  - Ensure the app allows for tenant-specific customizations.
  - Use configuration settings and extension points for flexibility.

CHAPTER 2   INSTALLATION, DEVELOPMENT, AND DEPLOYMENT FOR BUSINESS
            CENTRAL CHAPTER

- **Isolated Environments**
  - Deploy the app in isolated environments for each tenant to ensure data privacy and prevent cross-tenant data access.

Postdeployment Activities

- **Monitoring**
  - Monitor the app's performance and gather user feedback.
  - Use monitoring tools to track usage and identify issues.

- **Support**
  - Provide ongoing support to address user issues and queries.
  - Have a dedicated support team or helpdesk in place.

- **User Training**
  - Conduct training sessions for users to familiarize them with the new functionalities.
  - Provide comprehensive user documentation and tutorials.

- **Regular Maintenance**
  - Schedule regular maintenance checks and updates.
  - Apply security patches and feature updates as needed.

Rollback Strategy

- **Backup Restoration**
  - Have a backup restoration plan ready in case of deployment failures.
  - Test the backup restoration process periodically.

- **Revert Changes**
  - Be prepared to revert to a previous stable version if issues are identified post deployment.
  - Document the steps for reverting changes.

Best Practices

- **Automation**
  - Automate deployment tasks using scripts and tools to reduce manual errors.
  - Implement CI/CD pipelines for continuous integration and deployment.

- **Communication**
  - Communicate deployment schedules, potential downtime, and new features to users.
  - Ensure clear and timely communication to manage user expectations.

- **Compliance Checks**
  - Ensure the deployment complies with all regulatory and organizational policies.
  - Conduct periodic compliance audits.

Additional Resources

- Refer to the official Microsoft documentation for detailed guidance and best practices.
- Utilize available tools and resources for Business Central development and deployment.

Segment AL Code and Reduce Naming Conflicts with Namespaces

Namespaces in AL are essential for organizing code into logical groups and hierarchies, helping to prevent naming conflicts that occur when libraries are combined. By providing structure to the codebase, namespaces make it easier to navigate and understand, ensuring the uniqueness of code names and allowing the reuse of names in different contexts.

Declaring Namespaces

In AL, a namespace is declared at the beginning of a file, and all objects in that file belong to that namespace. While an object can only belong to one namespace, the same namespace can be used across multiple AL files. Here is how to declare a namespace:

```
namespace MyNamespace;
// codeunits, tables, pages...
```

This declaration groups all objects in the file under MyNamespace. You can use the same namespace in other files to logically group related objects.

Using the Namespace Keyword

To define a namespace, use the namespace keyword followed by the name of the namespace. Here are some best practices:

- **Globally Unique**: Ensure the namespace is globally unique.
- **Hierarchical Structure**: Use a structure that ties the namespace to the developing organization or product, like BigCompany.SmartProduct.SomeProductArea.
- **Stable Name**: Avoid changing the namespace name, as it can cause breaking changes.

Example of Namespace Declaration

```
namespace BigCompany.SmartProduct.SomeProductArea;
```

The Using Directive

To refer to objects in other namespaces without using the fully qualified name, use the using directive. This directive is placed at the top of the file, after the namespace declaration:

```
namespace MyNamespace;
using SomeOtherNamespace;
codeunit 10 MyCode
{
    // Code here can use objects from SomeOtherNamespace
    without fully qualifying the names
}
```

Nested Namespaces

Nested namespaces allow for better structured naming of objects. Here's an example of a nested namespace declaration:

```
namespace MyNamespace.MyNestedNamespace;
```

To refer to objects in MyNamespace.MyNestedNamespace, use the fully qualified name or the using directive:

```
using MyNamespace.MyNestedNamespace;
```

Managing Namespaces and Object Names

To avoid naming conflicts, each object must have a unique name within its namespace. Here are the key points:

- **One Object per Kind**: You can only have one object of a kind with the same name in a module or namespace.

- **Avoid Renaming**: Renaming existing objects or namespaces is a breaking change. Any dependent apps will break if a namespace is renamed.

Practical Tips for Namespaces

- **Prefix and Suffix**: Use a prefix or suffix to ensure object names are unique. Register your prefix/suffix with Microsoft by emailing d365val@microsoft.com.

- **Code Actions**: Use code actions in Visual Studio Code to help add namespaces to existing source files.

Example of Using Directives and Nested Namespaces

```
namespace BigCompany.SmartProduct.Sales;
using BigCompany.SmartProduct.Inventory;
codeunit 50100 SalesOperations
{
    // Code here can use objects from the Inventory namespace
    without fully qualifying the names
}
```

Integration with Microsoft Power Platform Products

Integrating Dynamics 365 Business Central with Microsoft Power Platform products can significantly enhance the capabilities and functionalities of your business processes. The Power Platform includes tools like Power BI, Power Apps, Power Automate, and Power Virtual Agents, each offering unique features to automate workflows, analyze data, create custom applications, and build intelligent bots.

1. Power BI Integration

Objective: Enhance data analysis and reporting capabilities.

- **Data Connectivity**: Connect Business Central to Power BI using default connectors to pull data and create insightful dashboards and reports. While these connectors provide a good starting point, some critical fields and columns may not be exposed by default.

- **Custom Data Exposure**: To access all necessary data, you may need to expose additional datasets using custom extensions. This ensures that critical information is available for comprehensive analytics. For more details, you can refer to `https://learn.microsoft.com/en-us/dynamics365/business-central/admin-powerbi-setup#exposedata`.

- **Embedded Reports**: Embed Power BI reports directly within Business Central to provide users with a seamless experience. This integration enables users to view and interact with detailed analytics without leaving the Business Central environment.

- **Prebuilt Content Packs**: Utilize prebuilt content packs and dashboards tailored for Business Central, providing a quick start to building comprehensive analytics.

Steps:

1. **Follow Recommended Process**: Begin by following the recommended process for integrating Power BI with Business Central. Detailed instructions can be found in `https://learn.microsoft.com/en-us/dynamics365/business-central/across-how-use-financials-data-source-powerbi`.

2. **Enable Power BI Integration**: Navigate to the Business Central setup and enable Power BI integration to start using data from your Business Central environment in Power BI.

3. **Connect Data**: Use the Power BI data connector for Business Central to connect your data. This connector is essential for linking your Business Central data with Power BI.

4. **Build Reports**: Create custom reports and dashboards in Power BI using Business Central data, leveraging the connected data to gain insights and improve decision-making.

5. **Embed Reports**: Embed the reports into Business Central pages for easy access, allowing users to view and interact with reports directly within the Business Central environment.

2. Power Apps Integration

Objective: Develop custom business applications without extensive coding.

- **Custom Apps**: Build custom applications tailored to specific business needs using Power Apps. These apps can interact with Business Central data, enabling users to perform tasks and access information from any device.

- **Canvas and Model-Driven Apps**: Create canvas apps for pixel-perfect designs or model-driven apps for data-centric applications, both of which can leverage Business Central data.

- **Common Data Service**: Utilize the Common Data Service (now known as Dataverse) to store and manage data used by Business Central and Power Apps, ensuring data consistency and integrity.

CHAPTER 2　INSTALLATION, DEVELOPMENT, AND DEPLOYMENT FOR BUSINESS CENTRAL CHAPTER

Steps:

1. **Set Up Environment**: Ensure you have a Power Apps environment set up and configured.

2. **Connect to Business Central**: Use the Business Central connector to link your data to Power Apps.

3. **Design and Build**: Use the Power Apps Studio to design and build your custom application.

4. **Deploy and Share**: Deploy the app within your organization and share it with relevant users.

3. Power Automate Integration

Objective: Automate workflows and business processes.

- **Automated Workflows**: Create automated workflows that integrate Business Central with other applications and services. Power Automate can handle repetitive tasks, such as approvals, notifications, and data updates, reducing manual effort.

- **Templates**: Use predefined templates to quickly set up common workflows involving Business Central, such as invoice approvals, customer follow-ups, and data synchronization.

- **Triggers and Actions**: Define triggers based on Business Central events (e.g., a new sales order) and specify actions (e.g., send an email notification).

Steps:

1. **Create a Flow**: Open Power Automate and create a new flow.

2. **Choose a Trigger**: Select a trigger from Business Central, such as a new record creation or update.

3. **Define Actions**: Add actions to be performed when the trigger condition is met, such as sending an email or updating another system.

4. **Test and Deploy**: Test the flow to ensure it works correctly and then deploy it within your organization.

Integration Checklist for Microsoft Power Platform Products

General Do's and Don'ts

Do's:

- **Set Up Accounts Properly**
  - Ensure all necessary accounts for Business Central and Power Platform products are created and configured.
  - Activate trial versions if needed.
- **Verify Permissions and Licensing**
  - Confirm that appropriate permissions and licenses are in place for all users involved in the integration.

CHAPTER 2   INSTALLATION, DEVELOPMENT, AND DEPLOYMENT FOR BUSINESS CENTRAL CHAPTER

- **Prepare Data**

    - Clean and structure Business Central data before integration.

    - Document data sources and necessary connectors.

- **Set Up Accounts Properly**: Ensure all necessary accounts for Business Central and Power Platform products are created and configured. Activate trial versions if needed.

- **Verify Permissions and Licensing**: Confirm that all required permissions are in place and that the correct licenses are assigned. Be mindful that while some licenses are fixed user-based subscriptions, others—like Power Automate—may be consumption-based, including data storage. It's essential to understand these to avoid unexpected usage-based charges.

Don'ts:

- **Avoid Skipping Sandbox Testing**

    - Do not bypass testing in a sandbox environment; always identify and resolve issues before moving to production.

- **Neglecting Backup Procedures**

    - Do not deploy without creating a full backup of the current production environment.

- **Overlooking Documentation**

    - Do not proceed without detailed documentation of the app's functionality, installation steps, and configuration settings.

CHAPTER 2 INSTALLATION, DEVELOPMENT, AND DEPLOYMENT FOR BUSINESS CENTRAL CHAPTER

Power BI Integration

Do's:

- **Enable Integration in Business Central**
  - Ensure Power BI integration is enabled in the Business Central setup.
- **Use Prebuilt Content Packs**
  - Utilize prebuilt content packs for a quick start on building comprehensive analytics.
- **Embed Reports**
  - Embed Power BI reports within Business Central for a seamless user experience.

Don'ts:

- **Ignoring Data Security Settings**
  - Do not ignore configuring data security and privacy settings during integration.
- **Neglecting Report Testing**
  - Do not skip testing reports to ensure they display accurate and updated data.

Power Apps Integration

Do's:

- **Set Up a Power Apps Environment**
  - Ensure the Power Apps environment is properly set up and configured.

CHAPTER 2   INSTALLATION, DEVELOPMENT, AND DEPLOYMENT FOR BUSINESS CENTRAL CHAPTER

- **Connect Data Properly**
    - Use the Business Central connector to link data accurately to Power Apps.
- **Leverage Canvas and Model-Driven Apps**
    - Choose the right type of app (canvas or model-driven) based on the specific requirements.

Don'ts:

- **Overcomplicate the Design**
    - Avoid overcomplicating the app design; keep it user-friendly and efficient.
- **Skipping Deployment Testing**
    - Do not deploy without thorough testing to ensure the app functions as intended.

Power Automate Integration

Do's:

- **Create Clear Workflows**
    - Design clear and efficient workflows to automate business processes.
- **Use Predefined Templates**
    - Utilize predefined templates to set up common workflows quickly.
- **Monitor and Optimize**
    - Continuously monitor workflows and optimize them based on performance and user feedback.

Don'ts:

- **Ignoring Error Handling**
  - Do not overlook implementing error handling in automated workflows.
- **Deploying Without Testing**
  - Do not deploy workflows without testing them thoroughly in a sandbox environment.

Power Virtual Agents Integration

Do's:

- **Design Effective Conversations**
  - Create clear and logical conversation flows to guide user interactions.
- **Integrate with Power Automate**
  - Use Power Automate to link the bot with Business Central data and actions.
- **Provide Comprehensive Training**
  - Train users on how to interact with the bot and understand its capabilities.

Don'ts:

- **Ignoring User Feedback**
  - Do not ignore user feedback; continuously improve the bot based on insights.
- **Deploying Without Testing**
  - Do not deploy the bot without thorough testing to ensure it handles queries correctly.

CHAPTER 2   INSTALLATION, DEVELOPMENT, AND DEPLOYMENT FOR BUSINESS CENTRAL CHAPTER

Postintegration Activities

Do's:

1. **Offer User Training and Documentation**
   - Provide training sessions and comprehensive documentation to users.

2. **Set Up Monitoring Tools**
   - Implement monitoring tools to track the performance of integrations and address any issues promptly.

3. **Schedule Regular Updates**
   - Plan regular updates and maintenance for all integrated solutions.

Don'ts:

1. **Neglecting Regular Maintenance**
   - Do not skip scheduled maintenance; keep the system up-to-date with the latest features and security patches.

2. **Overlooking User Communication**
   - Do not fail to communicate deployment schedules, potential downtime, and new features to users.

Conclusion

In this chapter, we have navigated through the essential processes of installation, development, and deployment within Dynamics 365 Business Central, with a particular emphasis on the sandbox environment.

CHAPTER 2   INSTALLATION, DEVELOPMENT, AND DEPLOYMENT FOR BUSINESS CENTRAL CHAPTER

The objective has been to equip you with the foundational knowledge and practical skills necessary to set up, customize, and deploy solutions effectively.

Key Takeaways

1. **Installation Procedures**: We began by discussing the setup of a sandbox environment, a crucial first step for developing and testing applications safely. You learned how to configure the sandbox environment, ensuring a secure and isolated space for experimentation without affecting the live production environment.

2. **Development Process**: We explored the development lifecycle, from designing solutions based on business requirements to developing and testing them using Visual Studio Code and the AL Language. You now understand how to create and deploy extensions, utilizing best practices to ensure robust and maintainable code.

3. **Deployment Strategies**: The chapter detailed strategic approaches to deploying Business Central apps, including packaging extensions, managing versions, and ensuring seamless updates. Emphasis was placed on incremental updates, thorough testing, and utilizing automation tools to streamline the deployment process.

4. **Integration with Microsoft Power Platform:** Integration capabilities with Power BI, Power Apps, Power Automate, and Power Virtual Agents were highlighted. These integrations enhance Business Central's functionality, enabling advanced data analysis, custom application development, automated workflows, and intelligent chatbots.

Exercise

Exercise 1: Setting Up a Sandbox Environment

Objective: Learn how to set up a sandbox environment in Dynamics 365 Business Central.

Steps:

1. Sign up for a Dynamics 365 Business Central sandbox environment here.

2. Download and install Visual Studio Code from the Visual Studio Code website.

3. Install the AL Language extension in Visual Studio Code.

4. Create a new AL project using the `AL: Go!` command and select the Microsoft cloud sandbox as the server.

5. Deploy a HelloWorld extension by pressing `Ctrl + F5`.

Expected Outcome:

- A functioning sandbox environment with a deployed HelloWorld extension.

Exercise 2: Building a Simple Extension

Objective: Create and deploy a simple extension in Business Central.

Steps:

1. Open Visual Studio Code and create a new AL project.

2. Define a new table and a page in AL.

3. Write AL code to implement a simple business logic, such as calculating the sum of two fields.

4. Deploy the extension to the sandbox environment.

Expected Outcome:

- A new table and page in Business Central that performs the specified business logic.

CHAPTER 3

AL Object Development in Business Central

This chapter provides a comprehensive exploration of AL (Application Language) objects in Dynamics 365 Business Central, aiming to equip readers with the knowledge and skills needed to create, modify, and manage AL objects effectively. The chapter is structured to offer a detailed understanding of various AL object types, practical steps for creating and modifying these objects, adherence to best practices, and efficient version control and management techniques.

We begin by understanding AL objects and their types, defining what AL objects are and their significance in Business Central. This includes an overview of different types of AL objects such as tables, pages, reports, codeunits, and queries, explaining the specific roles and use cases for each type within Business Central applications. This foundational knowledge sets the stage for more advanced topics.

Next, we delve into creating and modifying AL objects. This section starts with setting up the development environment, including steps to set up Visual Studio Code and necessary extensions for AL development. We provide a detailed guide on how to create different AL objects from scratch, complete with code examples and walkthroughs. Techniques for

CHAPTER 3   AL OBJECT DEVELOPMENT IN BUSINESS CENTRAL

modifying existing objects, ensuring backward compatibility, and avoiding conflicts are also covered. Hands-on examples and exercises are included to reinforce the creation and modification processes, providing practical experience to the readers.

The chapter then shifts to best practices for AL object development. We discuss recommended coding standards and conventions for writing clean, maintainable AL code, as well as tips and strategies for optimizing the performance of AL objects. Best practices for implementing robust error handling in AL code are also explored, alongside the importance of proper documentation and comments in the development process. This section ensures that readers not only know how to develop AL objects but also how to do so efficiently and effectively.

Finally, we address version control and management for AL objects. This begins with an introduction to version control and its importance in AL development. We provide an overview of tools like Git for version control, including setup and configuration. Techniques for effective branching and merging to manage development workflows are discussed, ensuring that readers can handle complex development scenarios. Best practices for managing extensions and updates are also included to ensure smooth deployment and maintenance.

This chapter also highlights the use of GitHub Copilot, a tool widely used by developers to assist with code writing and provide relevant code suggestions. While Copilot can enhance productivity, it is essential to use it with caution and review generated code thoroughly. Git also offers many prebuilt sample codes, which can be beneficial but should be used judiciously to ensure they fit the specific context of your project. Best practices for managing extensions and updates are also included to ensure smooth deployment and maintenance.

This chapter serves as a crucial resource for developers aiming to master the development of AL objects in Dynamics 365 Business Central, providing practical insights, best practices, and hands-on examples to enhance their proficiency and efficiency.

CHAPTER 3 AL OBJECT DEVELOPMENT IN BUSINESS CENTRAL

Introduction to AL Programming

AL (Application Language) is the programming language used for developing applications and customizations in Dynamics 365 Business Central. It is designed to be easy to read and write, allowing developers to create extensions and modify existing functionalities effectively. AL is closely integrated with Visual Studio Code, providing a robust environment for development with features like IntelliSense, debugging, and source control.

Types of AL Objects

AL objects are the building blocks of Business Central applications. They define the structure and behavior of data, user interfaces, and business logic. Here, we explore the main types of AL objects.

Tables in Dynamics 365 Business Central

Tables are a fundamental component in Dynamics 365 Business Central, serving as the primary data storage structure. They define the schema for data storage, including fields, data types, and relationships. Here is an in-depth look at tables, their properties, and their roles in Business Central.

Table Structure and Properties

Fields: Fields are the basic units of data storage within a table. Each field has a name, data type, and various properties that define its behavior and constraints. Common data types include Integer, Decimal, Date, Text, and Boolean. Fields can also have additional properties such as length, default values, and validation rules.

CHAPTER 3   AL OBJECT DEVELOPMENT IN BUSINESS CENTRAL

Keys: Keys are used to uniquely identify records within a table and to define sorting and indexing criteria. There are two main types of keys:

- **Primary Keys**: Uniquely identify each record in the table. Each table must have one primary key, which can consist of one or more fields.

- **Secondary Keys**: Provide additional sorting and searching capabilities. They are used to optimize queries and improve performance.

Triggers: Triggers are special procedures that are executed automatically in response to specific events on the table, such as inserting, modifying, or deleting records. Common triggers include

- **OnInsert**: Executed when a new record is inserted into the table

- **OnModify**: Executed when an existing record is modified

- **OnDelete**: Executed when a record is deleted from the table

- **OnRename**: Executed when a record's primary key is changed

Table Relations: Table relations define the relationships between tables, such as one-to-many or many-to-many relationships. These relationships are established using foreign keys, which reference primary keys in other tables. Table relations ensure data integrity and enforce referential constraints.

```
table 50100 Customer
{
    DataClassification = ToBeClassified;
    fields
```

```
    {
        field(1; CustomerID; Integer)
        {
            DataClassification = CustomerContent;
            Editable = false;
        }
        field(2; Name; Text[100])
        {
            DataClassification = CustomerContent;
        }
        field(3; Balance; Decimal)
        {
            DataClassification = Financial;
        }
    }

    keys
    {
        key(PK; CustomerID)
        {
            Clustered = true;
        }
    }

    trigger OnInsert()
    begin
        // Custom logic to execute when a new record is inserted
        // Custom logic to execute when a new record is inserted
        // Example: Call an approval workflow for the
        new customer record ApprovalWorkflowHandler.
        StartApprovalWorkflow(Rec);
    end;
}
```

CHAPTER 3   AL OBJECT DEVELOPMENT IN BUSINESS CENTRAL

Creating and Modifying Tables

Creating a new table in AL involves defining its structure, fields, keys, and triggers. Here's an example of a simple table definition.

In this example, the `Customer` table has three fields: `CustomerID`, `Name`, and `Balance`. The primary key is defined on the `CustomerID` field, and a trigger is included to execute custom logic when a new record is inserted.

Table Extensions

Table extensions allow developers to add new fields and functionality to existing tables without modifying the original table definition. This ensures that customizations are isolated and do not interfere with standard application updates. Here is an example of a table extension:

```
tableextension 50100 CustomerExtension extends Customer
{
    fields
    {
        field(50100; LoyaltyPoints; Integer)
        {
            DataClassification = ToBeClassified;
        }
    }

    trigger OnModify()
    begin
        // Custom logic to execute when a record is modified
    end;
}

tableextension 50100 CustomerExtension extends Customer
{
    fields
```

```
    {
        field(50100; LoyaltyPoints; Integer)
        {
            DataClassification = ToBeClassified;
        }
    }

    trigger OnModify()
    begin
        // Custom logic to execute when a record is modified
    end;
}
```

In this example, a new field `LoyaltyPoints` is added to the existing `Customer` table, and a trigger is defined to execute custom logic when a record is modified.

Best Practices for Table Design

- **Data Integrity**: Ensure that data integrity is maintained by defining appropriate primary and foreign keys.

- **Normalization**: Normalize data to reduce redundancy and improve efficiency.

- **Performance Optimization**: Use secondary keys to optimize query performance and indexing.

- **Validation and Constraints**: Implement validation rules and constraints to enforce data consistency.

- **Documentation**: Document table structures, fields, and relationships to facilitate maintenance and future development.

- **Default Values for Existing Data**: When extending tables, assign default values to new fields for existing data to prevent issues with null values. This practice helps maintain data consistency and prevents problems associated with incomplete or missing data in historical records.

Tables are the backbone of any Business Central application, providing the necessary structure for data storage and management. By understanding and effectively utilizing tables, developers can create robust and scalable solutions that meet the diverse needs of businesses.

Pages in Business Central

Pages in Dynamics 365 Business Central are the primary means of presenting and interacting with data. They define the user interface and determine how users view, enter, and modify data. Pages are designed to provide a consistent and intuitive experience across different devices and form factors. Here's an overview of different types of pages, their uses, and examples.

Types of Pages

1. **Card Pages**
2. **List Pages**
3. **Role Center Pages**
4. **Document Pages**
5. **Worksheet Pages**
6. **ListPart Pages**
7. **CardPart Pages**
8. **Confirmation Dialog Pages**
9. **Standard Dialog Pages**

CHAPTER 3   AL OBJECT DEVELOPMENT IN BUSINESS CENTRAL

1. Card Pages

Explanation: Card pages are used for detailed data entry and viewing a single record. They typically display all the fields of a single table row, allowing users to add, edit, or view detailed information.

When to Use: Use card pages when you need to display detailed information for a single record, such as a customer, vendor, or item.

Example:

```
page 50100 CustomerCard
{
    PageType = Card;
    SourceTable = Customer;
    ApplicationArea = All;
    Caption = 'Customer Card';

    layout
    {
        area(Content)
        {
            group(Group)
            {
                field("No."; "No.") { }
                field(Name; Name) { }
                field(Address; Address) { }
                field("Phone No."; "Phone No.") { }
                field("E-Mail"; "E-Mail") { }
            }
        }
    }
}
```

2. List Pages

Explanation: List pages display multiple records in a tabular format, allowing users to browse, sort, filter, and select records.

When to Use: Use list pages when you need to present a collection of records, such as a list of customers, vendors, or sales orders.

Example:

```
page 50101 CustomerList
{
    PageType = List;
    SourceTable = Customer;
    ApplicationArea = All;
    Caption = 'Customer List';

    layout
    {
        area(Content)
        {
            repeater(Group)
            {
                field("No."; "No.") { }
                field(Name; Name) { }
                field(Address; Address) { }
                field("Phone No."; "Phone No.") { }
            }
        }
    }
}
```

CHAPTER 3   AL OBJECT DEVELOPMENT IN BUSINESS CENTRAL

3. Role Center Pages

Explanation: Role center pages provide a dashboard-like interface tailored to specific user roles, aggregating relevant information, tasks, and insights.

When to Use: Use role center pages to create a central hub for users, giving them a quick overview of their key tasks, notifications, and activities.

Example:

```
page 50102 CustomerRoleCenter
{
    PageType = RoleCenter;
    ApplicationArea = All;
    Caption = 'Customer Role Center';

    layout
    {
        area(Content)
        {
            part(CustomerListPart; CustomerList) { }
            part(SalesOrderListPart; SalesOrderList) { }
        }
    }
}
```

4. Document Pages

Explanation: Document pages are used for transactions that involve multiple lines, such as sales orders, purchase orders, and invoices. They typically consist of a header section and a lines section.

When to Use: Use document pages for complex data entry forms where a single record involves multiple related entries, such as line items on an order.

CHAPTER 3   AL OBJECT DEVELOPMENT IN BUSINESS CENTRAL

Example:

```
page 50103 SalesOrder
{
    PageType = Document;
    SourceTable = "Sales Header";
    ApplicationArea = All;
    Caption = 'Sales Order';

    layout
    {
        area(Content)
        {
            group(Header)
            {
                field("No."; "No.") { }
                field("Customer No."; "Customer No.") { }
                field("Order Date"; "Order Date") { }
            }
            repeater(Lines)
            {
                field("Item No."; "Item No.") { }
                field(Quantity; Quantity) { }
                field("Unit Price"; "Unit Price") { }
            }
        }
    }
}
```

5. Worksheet Pages

Explanation: Worksheet pages are used for complex data entry and processing tasks, such as journal entries or budget worksheets. They support a variety of data entry and processing features.

When to Use: Use worksheet pages when you need to manage large sets of data that require frequent updates and processing, like financial journals.

Example:

```
page 50104 GeneralJournal
{
    PageType = Worksheet;
    SourceTable = "Gen. Journal Line";
    ApplicationArea = All;
    Caption = 'General Journal';

    layout
    {
        area(Content)
        {
            repeater(Lines)
            {
                field("Journal Template Name"; "Journal
                Template Name") { }
                field("Line No."; "Line No.") { }
                field(Description; Description) { }
                field(Amount; Amount) { }
            }
        }
    }
}
```

6. ListPart Pages

Explanation: ListPart pages are used as subpages within other pages to display a list of related records. They are typically used in card pages or document pages to show related line items.

When to Use: Use ListPart pages to embed a list of related records within a parent page, such as line items in a sales order.

Example:

```
page 50105 SalesOrderLinesPart
{
    PageType = ListPart;
    SourceTable = "Sales Line";
    ApplicationArea = All;
    Caption = 'Sales Order Lines';

    layout
    {
        area(Content)
        {
            repeater(Lines)
            {
                field("Item No."; "Item No.") { }
                field(Quantity; Quantity) { }
                field("Unit Price"; "Unit Price") { }
            }
        }
    }
}
```

7. CardPart Pages

Explanation: CardPart pages are used to display detailed information for a single record within another page. They are typically used in role center or list pages to show additional details.

When to Use: Use CardPart pages to provide detailed information about a selected record within a parent page.

Example:

```
page 50106 CustomerCardPart
{
    PageType = CardPart;
    SourceTable = Customer;
    ApplicationArea = All;
    Caption = 'Customer Details';

    layout
    {
        area(Content)
        {
            group(Group)
            {
                field("No."; "No.") { }
                field(Name; Name) { }
                field(Address; Address) { }
                field("Phone No."; "Phone No.") { }
                field("E-Mail"; "E-Mail") { }
            }
        }
    }
}
```

8. Confirmation Dialog Pages

Explanation: Confirmation dialog pages are used to prompt the user for confirmation before performing an action. They typically present a message and buttons for the user to confirm or cancel.

When to Use: Use confirmation dialog pages when you need to ensure the user intentionally wants to perform a specific action, such as deleting a record or submitting a transaction.

Example:

```
page 50107 ConfirmDeleteCustomer
{
    PageType = ConfirmationDialog;
    ApplicationArea = All;
    Caption = 'Confirm Delete Customer';

    layout
    {
        area(Content)
        {
            group(Group)
            {
                field(ConfirmationMessage; Text)
                {
                    ApplicationArea = All;
                    Caption = 'Are you sure you want to delete
                    this customer?';
                    Editable = false;
                }
            }
        }
    }
}
```

```
    actions
    {
        area(Action)
        {
            action(Confirm)
            {
                Caption = 'Yes';
                trigger OnAction()
                begin
                    // Perform delete action
                end;
            }
            action(Cancel)
            {
                Caption = 'No';
                trigger OnAction()
                begin
                    // Cancel action
                end;
            }
        }
    }
}
```

9. Standard Dialog Pages

Explanation: Standard dialog pages are used to collect user input through a series of fields, typically for quick and simple data entry tasks.

When to Use: Use standard dialog pages when you need to prompt the user for input or parameters, such as setting filters or entering configuration settings.

CHAPTER 3   AL OBJECT DEVELOPMENT IN BUSINESS CENTRAL

Example:

```
page 50108 SetReportParameters
{
    PageType = StandardDialog;
    ApplicationArea = All;
    Caption = 'Set Report Parameters';

    layout
    {
        area(Content)
        {
            group(Group)
            {
                field(StartDate; Date)
                {
                    ApplicationArea = All;
                    Caption = 'Start Date';
                }
                field(EndDate; Date)
                {
                    ApplicationArea = All;
                    Caption = 'End Date';
                }
            }
        }
    }
}
```

Each type of page in Business Central serves a specific purpose and provides a different way to interact with data. Understanding when and how to use these pages effectively is crucial for creating user-friendly and efficient applications. By mastering these various page types, developers can ensure that their applications meet the needs of end users while maintaining a consistent and intuitive interface.

Reports in Business Central

Reports in Dynamics 365 Business Central are used to format and present data in a printable and readable format. They are essential for generating documents like invoices, purchase orders, and financial statements. Reports can include complex data manipulations and calculations and can be customized to fit specific business needs.

Report Structure and Properties

Data Items: Data items are the core elements of a report, defining the tables from which data is retrieved. Each data item corresponds to a table or a part of a table and can be linked to other data items to form hierarchical data structures.

Sections: Reports are divided into different sections where the layout and presentation of data are defined. These sections include

- **Header**: Contains information that appears at the top of each page, such as titles and logos.

- **Body**: The main section where the data is displayed. It includes data fields, text boxes, and graphics.

- **Footer**: Contains information that appears at the bottom of each page, such as page numbers and summaries.

CHAPTER 3   AL OBJECT DEVELOPMENT IN BUSINESS CENTRAL

Triggers: Triggers are AL code units that are executed at specific events during report generation. Common triggers include

- **OnInitReport**: Executed when the report is initialized
- **OnPreDataItem**: Executed before data is retrieved for a data item
- **OnAfterGetRecord**: Executed after each record is retrieved
- **OnPostReport**: Executed after the report is generated

Creating a Simple Report

Here's an example of a simple report that lists customers and their balances:

```
report 50100 CustomerBalance
{
    ApplicationArea = All;
    Caption = 'Customer Balance Report';

    dataset
    {
        dataitem(Customer; Customer)
        {
            column(Name; Name) { }
            column(Balance; "Balance (LCY)") { }
        }
    }

    requestpage
    {
        layout
        {
```

```
            area(Content)
            {
                group(Group)
                {
                    field(CustomerName; Name) { }
                    field(CustomerBalance; "Balance (LCY)") { }
                }
            }
        }
    }
    layout
    {
        area(header)
        {
            textbox(Title)
            {
                Value = 'Customer Balance Report';
                Style = Title;
            }
        }

        area(content)
        {
            dataitem(Customer)
            {
                column(CustomerName; Name) { }
                column(CustomerBalance; "Balance (LCY)") { }
            }
        }
```

CHAPTER 3   AL OBJECT DEVELOPMENT IN BUSINESS CENTRAL

```
        area(footer)
        {
            textbox(PageNumber)
            {
                Value = 'Page ' + FORMAT(CurrReport.PAGENO);
                Style = PageNumber;
            }
        }
    }
}
```

In this example

- The **dataset** section defines the data items and columns that will be included in the report.

- The **requestpage** section defines the layout of the request page where users can set parameters.

- The **layout** section defines the visual layout of the report, including the header, body, and footer.

Report Extension

Report extensions allow developers to extend existing reports by adding new data items, columns, and layout changes without modifying the original report. This ensures customizations are isolated and do not interfere with standard application updates.

Example:

```
reportextension 50101 CustomerBalanceExtension extends "Customer Balance Report"
{
    dataset
    {
```

```
        dataitem(Customer)
        {
            column(CreditLimit; "Credit Limit (LCY)") { }
        }
    }
    layout
    {
        modify(Customer)
        {
            addafter(CustomerBalance)
            {
                column(CreditLimit; "Credit Limit (LCY)") { }
            }
        }
    }
}
```

In this example, a new column `Credit Limit (LCY)` is added to the existing `Customer Balance Report` without altering the original report.

Best Practices for Report Design

- **Performance Optimization**: Minimize the number of data items and ensure efficient data retrieval to optimize report performance.

- **User-Friendly Layout**: Design reports with a clear and logical layout to make them easy to read and understand.

- **Validation and Error Handling**: Implement validation and error handling to ensure data integrity and report accuracy.

- **Documentation**: Document the report structure, data items, and layout to facilitate maintenance and future development.

- **Reusability**: Use report extensions to customize and extend reports without duplicating or modifying the original reports.

Reports in Business Central are powerful tools for data presentation and analysis. By understanding the structure and capabilities of reports, developers can create comprehensive and customizable reports that meet the specific needs of businesses, ensuring that critical information is presented accurately and effectively.

Codeunits in Business Central

Codeunits in Dynamics 365 Business Central are AL objects that contain business logic and procedures. They are used to encapsulate reusable code, making it easier to manage and maintain. Codeunits can contain functions, triggers, and event subscribers, allowing developers to modularize and organize their application logic.

Introduction to Codeunits

Codeunits are akin to classes in object-oriented programming. They encapsulate methods (procedures) that can be called from other AL objects like pages, reports, and other codeunits. This modular approach promotes code reuse and helps in maintaining clean and manageable codebases.

Key Features of Codeunits:

- Encapsulation of business logic
- Reusability across different parts of the application

- Organization and modularization of code
- Simplification of maintenance and updates

Common Use Cases:
- Complex calculations
- Data manipulation and processing
- Integrations with external systems
- Handling business processes

Creating a Codeunit

Creating a codeunit involves defining a new AL object and writing the required procedures. Here's a step-by-step guide to creating a simple codeunit in AL.

Step 1: Define the Codeunit

To define a new codeunit, use the codeunit keyword followed by a unique ID and a name for the codeunit.

```
codeunit 50100 MyCodeunit
{
    Caption = 'My Codeunit';
}
```

Step 2: Add Procedures

Add procedures within the codeunit to encapsulate your business logic. Procedures can be local (accessible only within the codeunit) or global (accessible from other objects).

```
codeunit 50100 MyCodeunit
{
    Caption = 'My Codeunit';
```

```al
        procedure CalculateSum(a: Integer; b: Integer): Integer
        begin
            exit(a + b);
        end;
}
```

In this example, the `CalculateSum` procedure takes two integers as input and returns their sum.

Step 3: Calling Procedures

You can call the procedures defined in a codeunit from other AL objects. First, declare a variable of the codeunit type and then call the procedure using this variable.

```al
page 50100 TestPage
{
    PageType = Card;
    ApplicationArea = All;
    Caption = 'Test Page';

    var
        MyCodeunitInstance: Codeunit MyCodeunit;

    layout
    {
        area(Content)
        {
            group(Group)
            {
                field(Result; Integer)
                {
                    Editable = false;
                }
            }
```

CHAPTER 3 AL OBJECT DEVELOPMENT IN BUSINESS CENTRAL

```
            }
        }
        actions
        {
            area(Processing)
            {
                action(Calculate)
                {
                    Caption = 'Calculate';
                    trigger OnAction()
                    begin
                        Result := MyCodeunitInstance.
                        CalculateSum(10, 20);
                    end;
                }
            }
        }
        var
            Result: Integer;
}
```

In this example, the `Calculate` action calls the `CalculateSum` procedure from the `MyCodeunit` codeunit and displays the result "30" on the page.

Event-Driven Programming with Codeunits

Codeunits can also be used to handle events. This allows for a decoupled design where different parts of the application can react to changes or actions without being directly connected.

Subscribing to Events

To subscribe to an event, define a procedure in a codeunit and decorate it with the `EventSubscriber` attribute.

```
codeunit 50101 MyEventSubscriber
{
    [EventSubscriber(ObjectType::Table, Database::Customer,
    'OnAfterInsertEvent', '', false, false)]
    procedure OnAfterCustomerInsert(var Rec: Record Customer)
    begin
        Message('Customer %1 was inserted.', Rec.Name);
    end;
}
```

In this example, the `OnAfterCustomerInsert` procedure is called after a customer record is inserted, displaying a message with the customer's name.

Best Practices for Codeunit Development

1. **Modularization**: Break down complex business logic into smaller, reusable procedures.
2. **Naming Conventions**: Use clear and consistent naming conventions for codeunits and procedures.
3. **Documentation**: Document the purpose and usage of codeunits and their procedures.
4. **Error Handling**: Implement robust error handling within procedures to ensure reliability.
5. **Testing**: Thoroughly test codeunits and their interactions with other AL objects to ensure correctness and performance.

Example of a Complete Codeunit

Below is an example of a complete codeunit that includes multiple procedures and demonstrates different functionalities.

```
codeunit 50102 ExampleCodeunit
{
    Caption = 'Example Codeunit';

    procedure CalculateSum(a: Integer; b: Integer): Integer
    begin
        exit(a + b);
    end;

    procedure MultiplyNumbers(a: Integer; b: Integer): Integer
    begin
        exit(a * b);
    end;

    procedure SendNotification(MessageText: Text[100])
    begin
        Notification.CreateNotification('Notification',
        MessageText, true);
    end;

    [EventSubscriber(ObjectType::Table, Database::SalesHeader,
    'OnAfterInsertEvent', '', false, false)]
    procedure OnAfterSalesHeaderInsert(var Rec: Record "Sales
    Header")
    begin
        Message('Sales order %1 was inserted.', Rec."No.");
    end;
}
```

This codeunit includes

- `CalculateSum` and `MultiplyNumbers` procedures for arithmetic operations
- `SendNotification` procedure for sending notifications
- An event subscriber for the `Sales Header` table that displays a message after a sales order is inserted

Codeunits in Business Central are powerful tools for encapsulating business logic and ensuring code reusability and maintainability. By leveraging codeunits effectively, developers can create robust and scalable applications that meet complex business requirements.

Queries in Business Central

Queries in Dynamics 365 Business Central are AL objects designed to retrieve data from one or more tables in a structured way. They allow developers to define complex data retrieval logic, including filtering, sorting, and joining tables, which can then be used in reports, pages, or other AL objects.

Key Concepts and Structure

>**Data Items**: The primary building blocks of a query. Each data item represents a table from which data is retrieved. Data items can be linked to each other to form complex data structures.
>
>**Columns**: Columns specify the fields to be included in the query results. They are defined within each data item and can include calculations, expressions, and aggregations.

CHAPTER 3   AL OBJECT DEVELOPMENT IN BUSINESS CENTRAL

Filters: Filters are used to restrict the data retrieved by a query. They can be applied to any column to include only the records that meet specific criteria.

Sorting: Sorting defines the order in which the query results are returned. Sorting can be applied to any column to organize the data in ascending or descending order.

Creating a Simple Query

Here's an example of a simple query that retrieves customer names and their balance:

```
query 50100 CustomerBalanceQuery
{
    DataItem(Customer; Customer)
    {
        Column(Name; Name)
        {
            DataType = Text;
        }
        Column(Balance; "Balance (LCY)")
        {
            DataType = Decimal;
        }
    }
}
```

CHAPTER 3 AL OBJECT DEVELOPMENT IN BUSINESS CENTRAL

In this example

- The DataItem element defines the Customer table as the source of data.

- Two Column elements specify the fields to include in the results: Name and Balance (LCY).

Advanced Query Example with Joins and Filters

Here's a more advanced query that joins the Customer and Sales Invoice Header tables and includes filters:

```
query 50101 CustomerSalesQuery
{
    DataItem(Customer; Customer)
    {
        Column(Name; Name)
        {
            DataType = Text;
        }
        DataItem(SalesInvoice; "Sales Invoice Header")
        {
            DataItemLink = "Customer No." = field("No.");

            Column(SalesAmount; Amount)
            {
                DataType = Decimal;
            }
            Column(SalesDate; "Posting Date")
            {
                DataType = Date;
            }
```

```
            Filter(SalesDate; "Posting Date")
            {
                DataType = Date;
                FilterExpression = '%1..%2';
            }
        }
    }
}
```

In this example

- The Customer data item is the primary source.
- The Sales Invoice Header data item is linked to the Customer data item through the DataItemLink property.
- Columns from both tables are included in the results.
- A filter is applied to the SalesDate column to restrict the data retrieved.

Using Queries in AL Code

Queries can be used in AL code to retrieve and process data. Here's an example of how to use a query in a codeunit:

```
codeunit 50102 ProcessCustomerSales
{
    procedure GetCustomerSales()
    var
        CustomerSalesQuery: Query CustomerSalesQuery;
        Name: Text[100];
        SalesAmount: Decimal;
        SalesDate: Date;
```

```al
begin
    CustomerSalesQuery.SetFilter("SalesDate",
    '01/01/2023..31/12/2023');
    if CustomerSalesQuery.Open then begin
        while CustomerSalesQuery.Read do begin
            Name := CustomerSalesQuery.Name;
            SalesAmount := CustomerSalesQuery.SalesAmount;
            SalesDate := CustomerSalesQuery.SalesDate;
            // Process the retrieved data
        end;
    end;
    CustomerSalesQuery.Close;
end;
}
```

In this example

- The `CustomerSalesQuery` query is used to retrieve sales data for customers.
- The `SetFilter` method applies a date range filter to the query.
- The `Open` method runs the query, and the `Read` method iterates through the results.
- The retrieved data is processed within the loop.

Best Practices for Queries

1. **Optimize Performance**: Use filters and joins efficiently to minimize the data retrieved and improve query performance.

2. **Modular Design**: Create reusable queries that can be utilized across different AL objects to maintain consistency and reduce duplication.

3. **Error Handling**: Implement error handling to manage exceptions and ensure the robustness of your queries.

4. **Documentation**: Document the purpose, structure, and usage of your queries to facilitate maintenance and future development.

5. **Testing**: Thoroughly test queries to ensure they return the correct data and perform well under different conditions.

Best Practices for AL Object Development

Developing AL objects for Dynamics 365 Business Central requires a methodical approach to ensure efficiency, maintainability, and performance. Below are best practices to follow for AL object development:

1. Modularization and Reusability

- **Encapsulate Logic in Codeunits**: Use codeunits to encapsulate business logic and reusable code. This promotes code reuse and simplifies maintenance.
- **Use Extensions**: Leverage table, page, and report extensions to add functionality without modifying the base application, making upgrades easier.

2. Naming Conventions

- **Consistent Naming**: Use clear, descriptive, and consistent naming conventions for all AL objects, fields, variables, and methods. This improves readability and maintainability.

- **Prefixes and Suffixes**: Apply prefixes or suffixes to custom objects to avoid naming conflicts with base application objects. For example, use MyCompany_ as a prefix for custom tables and pages.

3. Documentation and Comments

- **Document Your Code**: Provide detailed comments and documentation for complex logic, function parameters, return values, and important code sections. This helps other developers understand your code and facilitates future maintenance.

- **AL Documentation Comments**: Use XML documentation comments for methods and properties to provide inline documentation that is accessible in the development environment.

4. Version Control

- **Source Control Integration**: Use version control systems (e.g., Git) to manage changes to your AL codebase. This allows for tracking changes, collaboration, and rollback if necessary.

- **Frequent Commits**: Make small, frequent commits with clear commit messages to maintain a detailed history of changes.

5. Error Handling and Logging

- **Robust Error Handling**: Implement comprehensive error handling in your AL code to manage exceptions and ensure the reliability of your application.
- **Logging Mechanism**: Use logging mechanisms to record important events, errors, and application states. This aids in debugging and monitoring the application in production environments.

6. Performance Optimization

- **Efficient Data Access**: Optimize data access by using appropriate filters, indexes, and query structures to minimize the data retrieved and processed.
- **Avoid Unnecessary Calculations**: Minimize the use of complex calculations and loops within trigger events and frequently called methods to improve performance.
- **Batch Processing**: Implement batch processing for long-running operations to avoid performance bottlenecks and improve user experience.

7. Security

- **Permission Sets**: Define and assign appropriate permission sets to control access to AL objects and data. This ensures that users have the necessary permissions to perform their tasks.

- **Data Validation**: Implement data validation checks to ensure that only valid data is processed and stored.

8. Testing and Quality Assurance

- **Unit Testing**: Write unit tests for critical business logic to ensure correctness and prevent regressions. Use the AL test framework to create automated tests.

- **Code Review**: Conduct regular code reviews to ensure code quality, consistency, and adherence to best practices.

- **Continuous Integration**: Set up continuous integration (CI) pipelines to automatically build, test, and deploy your AL code. This helps catch issues early and ensures code quality.

9. User Experience

- **User-Friendly Interfaces**: Design user-friendly pages and reports with intuitive layouts, clear labels, and helpful tooltips. Ensure that navigation and actions are straightforward.

- **Accessibility**: Consider accessibility features to make your application usable by people with disabilities. This includes support for keyboard navigation, screen readers, and high-contrast themes.

10. Maintainability

- **Code Refactoring**: Regularly refactor code to improve structure, readability, and performance. Remove redundant code and simplify complex logic.

- **Consistent Style**: Follow a consistent coding style and guidelines to make the codebase uniform and easier to read.

Example of Best Practices in Action

Here's a sample codeunit that demonstrates several best practices:

```
codeunit 50100 MyExampleCodeunit
{
    Caption = 'My Example Codeunit';

    procedure CalculateDiscountedPrice(OriginalPrice: Decimal;
    DiscountRate: Decimal): Decimal
    begin
        if DiscountRate < 0 or DiscountRate > 100 then
            Error('Discount rate must be between 0 and 100.');

        exit(OriginalPrice * (1 - DiscountRate / 100));
    end;
```

```
procedure LogTransaction(TransactionId: Integer; Amount:
Decimal)
begin
    // Example logging
    Message('Transaction ID: %1, Amount: %2',
    TransactionId, Amount);
end;
}
```

Explanation

- **Modularization**: Business logic is encapsulated in a codeunit.

- **Error Handling**: Validation is performed on the discount rate to ensure it is within an acceptable range.

- **Logging**: A simple logging mechanism is used to display transaction details.

- **Comments and Documentation**: Comments provide context for code sections.

Additional Best Practice: Cohesion and Coupling

- **Cohesion**: Aim for high cohesion within AL objects, ensuring that all components of a module work together toward a single purpose. This improves clarity and makes the code easier to understand and maintain.

- **Coupling**: Strive for low coupling between modules, meaning that modules should be loosely coupled and interact with minimal dependencies. Use events, publishers/subscribers, or interfaces to achieve loose coupling, allowing for more flexible and modular extensions.

Checklist for Best Practices for AL Object Development

Modularization and Reusability

- **Encapsulate Business Logic**: Use codeunits to encapsulate business logic and reusable code.
- **Use Extensions**: Leverage table, page, and report extensions for adding functionality without modifying the base application.

Naming Conventions

- **Consistent Naming**: Use clear, descriptive, and consistent naming conventions for all AL objects, fields, variables, and methods.
- **Prefixes and Suffixes**: Apply prefixes or suffixes to custom objects to avoid naming conflicts with base application objects.

Documentation and Comments

- **Document Your Code**: Provide detailed comments and documentation for complex logic, function parameters, return values, and important code sections.
- **XML Documentation**: Use XML documentation comments for methods and properties to provide inline documentation.

Version Control

- **Source Control Integration**: Use version control systems (e.g., Git) to manage changes to your AL codebase.
- **Frequent Commits**: Make small, frequent commits with clear commit messages.

Error Handling and Logging

- **Robust Error Handling**: Implement comprehensive error handling in your AL code.
- **Logging Mechanism**: Use logging mechanisms to record important events, errors, and application states.

Performance Optimization

- **Efficient Data Access**: Optimize data access by using appropriate filters, indexes, and query structures.
- **Avoid Unnecessary Calculations**: Minimize complex calculations and loops within trigger events and frequently called methods.
- **Batch Processing**: Implement batch processing for long-running operations.

Security

- **Permission Sets**: Define and assign appropriate permission sets to control access to AL objects and data.

- **Data Validation**: Implement data validation checks to ensure only valid data is processed and stored.

Testing and Quality Assurance

- **Unit Testing**: Write unit tests for critical business logic using the AL test framework.

- **Code Review**: Conduct regular code reviews to ensure code quality and consistency.

- **Continuous Integration**: Set up CI pipelines to automatically build, test, and deploy your AL code.

User Experience

- **User-Friendly Interfaces**: Design user-friendly pages and reports with intuitive layouts, clear labels, and helpful tooltips.

- **Accessibility**: Consider accessibility features to make your application usable by people with disabilities.

CHAPTER 3 AL OBJECT DEVELOPMENT IN BUSINESS CENTRAL

Maintainability

- **Code Refactoring**: Regularly refactor code to improve structure, readability, and performance.

- **Consistent Style**: Follow a consistent coding style and guidelines.

Specific AL Object Best Practices

Tables

Use primary keys and indexes to optimize data retrieval.

Define appropriate field types and sizes.

Implement table relations and triggers carefully to maintain data integrity.

Pages

Design user-friendly interfaces with clear navigation.

Use appropriate page types (e.g., List, Card, Document) based on the use case.

Implement actions and validations to enhance user interactions.

Reports

Design reports to be clear and informative.

Use datasets and request pages to provide flexibility in report generation.

Optimize report performance by retrieving only necessary data.

CHAPTER 3   AL OBJECT DEVELOPMENT IN BUSINESS CENTRAL

Codeunits

Encapsulate reusable business logic.

Ensure codeunits are modular and follow single responsibility principle.

Handle exceptions and log errors appropriately.

Queries

Optimize queries for performance by using filters and joins efficiently.

Design queries to retrieve only the required data.

Test queries thoroughly to ensure accuracy and performance.

XMLPorts

Use XMLPorts for data import/export operations.

Define data structures clearly.

Handle errors and exceptions during data processing.

Extensions (Table/Page/Report)

Use extensions to add new functionality without modifying base objects.

Ensure compatibility with base application and other extensions.

Follow upgrade best practices to maintain extension functionality.

CHAPTER 3   AL OBJECT DEVELOPMENT IN BUSINESS CENTRAL

Version Control and Management for AL Objects

Version control is a critical aspect of managing your AL objects in Dynamics 365 Business Central, ensuring that changes are tracked, managed, and deployed efficiently. This section will provide an overview of best practices and tools for version control and management of AL objects.

Source Control Integration

Integrating a version control system (VCS) into your development workflow is essential. Git is a popular choice due to its robustness and widespread adoption.

- **Repository Setup**: Create repositories for your projects, structured in a way that suits your team's needs. Ensure repositories are accessible to the entire development team.
- **Branching Strategy**: Implement a branching strategy that aligns with your development workflow. Common strategies include Gitflow, feature branching, and trunk-based development.

Branching Strategy

A well-defined branching strategy helps manage parallel development efforts and streamline the integration process.

- **Main Branch**: The main (or master) branch should contain stable, production-ready code. Only thoroughly tested code should be merged here.
- **Development Branch**: The development branch integrates new features and bug fixes before they are merged into the main branch.

- **Feature Branches**: Create feature branches for individual features or bug fixes. These branches are short-lived and merged into the development branch once the feature is complete and tested.

Commit Practices

Effective commit practices are vital for maintaining a clear and manageable codebase.

- **Frequent Commits**: Commit changes frequently to capture the development process and make tracking easier.
- **Clear Commit Messages**: Use clear, concise, and descriptive commit messages to explain the purpose of each change.
- **Atomic Commits**: Ensure commits are atomic, meaning they represent a single, logical change to the codebase.

Pull Requests and Code Reviews

Using pull requests and conducting code reviews helps ensure code quality and facilitates collaboration.

- **Use Pull Requests**: Pull requests enable team members to review changes before they are merged into the main codebase.
- **Code Reviews**: Conduct thorough code reviews to ensure adherence to coding standards and best practices.

- **Automated Checks**: Integrate automated checks (e.g., linting, unit tests) into the pull request process to catch issues early.

Branch Merging

Merging branches effectively helps maintain a clean and functional codebase.

- **Merge Strategy**: Adopt a consistent merge strategy (e.g., squash and merge, rebase and merge) to maintain a clean commit history.
- **Resolve Conflicts**: Address conflicts promptly and correctly when merging branches.
- **Post-merge Testing**: Perform testing after merging to ensure that changes have not introduced any issues.

Tagging and Versioning

Tagging and versioning help track specific points in the repository history and manage releases.

- **Tag Releases**: Use tags to mark specific points in the repository history as releases, making it easier to track and deploy specific versions.
- **Semantic Versioning**: Follow semantic versioning (e.g., MAJOR.MINOR.PATCH) to indicate the significance of changes.

Continuous Integration and Deployment (CI/CD)

Implementing CI/CD pipelines automates the building, testing, and deployment processes.

- **CI Pipeline**: Set up a CI pipeline to automatically build, test, and validate changes on every commit or pull request.

- **Automated Tests**: Ensure that automated tests are part of the CI pipeline to catch issues early.

- **Deployment Pipeline**: Implement a deployment pipeline to automate the deployment of changes to different environments (e.g., development, staging, production). Azure DevOps offers comprehensive tools for managing deployment pipelines, ensuring smooth transitions between environments.

Backup and Recovery

Having a backup and recovery plan in place is essential to prevent data loss and ensure business continuity.

- **Regular Backups**: Schedule regular backups of your repositories to prevent data loss.

- **Recovery Plan**: Have a recovery plan in place to restore the repository in case of data loss or corruption.

CHAPTER 3   AL OBJECT DEVELOPMENT IN BUSINESS CENTRAL

Documentation and Training

Providing proper documentation and training helps ensure that all team members follow best practices and processes.

- **Version Control Guidelines**: Document version control guidelines and best practices for the development team.

- **Training**: Provide training for team members on using version control systems and following the defined processes.

GitHub Copilot

GitHub Copilot is an AI-powered code completion tool developed by GitHub in collaboration with OpenAI. It uses machine learning models trained on a vast amount of public code to suggest code snippets, function completions, and even entire functions as you type.

To use GitHub Copilot in Visual Studio Code

1. Install the GitHub Copilot extension from the VS Code marketplace.

2. Sign in to your GitHub account within VS Code.

3. Once activated, Copilot will start providing suggestions as you code.

As for using GitHub Copilot with Business Central, there are a few things to note:

1. Copilot can assist with AL code, which is used for Business Central development.

2. It can help with common patterns in AL, such as page and table object definitions, report layouts, and codeunit functions.

3. However, Copilot's suggestions for Business Central-specific code might not always be up-to-date or fully accurate, as it depends on the training data available.

4. Be cautious when using generated code for sensitive business logic or data handling in Business Central applications.

5. Always review and test Copilot's suggestions thoroughly before implementing them in your Business Central projects.

Conclusion

In this chapter, we delved into the essentials of AL object development in Dynamics 365 Business Central. We began by understanding the various AL object types, such as tables, pages, reports, codeunits, and queries, each serving a unique purpose in the application development lifecycle. By exploring the creation and modification of these objects, we gained insights into the practical aspects of building and extending Business Central functionalities.

We emphasized the importance of adhering to best practices in AL object development to ensure code quality, maintainability, and performance. These practices, ranging from consistent naming conventions to efficient data handling and modular design, are crucial for developing robust and scalable solutions.

Moreover, the chapter highlighted the significance of effective version control and management. Implementing a structured version control strategy, complete with branching, committing, and merging practices, ensures smooth collaboration and efficient handling of code changes. Integrating CI/CD pipelines further enhances the development process by automating build, test, and deployment tasks, leading to quicker and more reliable releases.

By following these guidelines and leveraging the tools and techniques discussed, you can master AL object development in Business Central, creating solutions that meet business requirements while maintaining high standards of code quality and manageability.

Key Takeaways from This Chapter

1. **Understanding AL Objects**

    - Gained a comprehensive understanding of the various AL objects in Dynamics 365 Business Central, including tables, pages, reports, codeunits, and queries.

    - Recognized the distinct roles and functionalities of each AL object type and how they contribute to the overall system.

2. **Creating and Modifying AL Objects**

    - Learned the processes for creating and modifying AL objects to customize and extend Business Central functionalities.

    - Explored practical examples and scenarios for developing different types of AL objects.

CHAPTER 3   AL OBJECT DEVELOPMENT IN BUSINESS CENTRAL

3. **Best Practices for AL Object Development**

    - Emphasized the importance of following best practices in AL object development to ensure code quality, maintainability, and performance.

    - Covered key practices such as consistent naming conventions, modular design, efficient data handling, and comprehensive testing.

4. **Version Control and Management**

    - Understood the critical role of version control in managing AL object development.

    - Implemented effective version control strategies, including branching, committing, merging, and tagging.

    - Integrated continuous integration and deployment (CI/CD) pipelines to automate build, test, and deployment processes.

5. **Collaboration and Quality Assurance**

    - Recognized the value of collaborative development practices such as pull requests and code reviews to ensure high code quality and consistency.

    - Leveraged automated checks and testing to catch issues early in the development process.

6. **Documentation and Training**:

    - Highlighted the necessity of maintaining proper documentation and providing training for the development team to follow best practices and version control processes.

Exercises for Chapter 3: AL Object Development in Business Central

Exercise 1: Create a Table

1. **Objective**: Create a new table to store customer feedback.

2. **Steps**

    - Open Visual Studio Code and create a new AL project.

    - Define a new table named CustomerFeedback.

    - Add fields for FeedbackID (Integer, primary key), CustomerID (Code[20]), FeedbackDate (Date), and Comments (Text[250]).

    - Set appropriate properties for each field (e.g., DataClassification, Caption).

Exercise 2: Create a Card Page

1. **Objective**: Create a card page to view and edit customer feedback.

2. **Steps**

    - Create a new page named CustomerFeedbackCard.

    - Set the PageType to Card and the SourceTable to CustomerFeedback.

    - Define the layout with groups and fields for FeedbackID, CustomerID, FeedbackDate, and Comments.

CHAPTER 3   AL OBJECT DEVELOPMENT IN BUSINESS CENTRAL

Answer

Exercise 1

```
table 50100 "CustomerFeedback"
{
    DataClassification = ToBeClassified;
    fields
    {
        field(1; "FeedbackID"; Integer)
        {
            DataClassification = ToBeClassified;
            AutoIncrement = true;
            Caption = 'Feedback ID';
        }
        field(2; "CustomerID"; Code[20])
        {
            DataClassification = ToBeClassified;
            Caption = 'Customer ID';
        }
        field(3; "FeedbackDate"; Date)
        {
            DataClassification = ToBeClassified;
            Caption = 'Feedback Date';
        }
        field(4; "Comments"; Text[250])
        {
            DataClassification = ToBeClassified;
            Caption = 'Comments';
        }
    }
}
```

```
    keys
    {
        key(PK; "FeedbackID")
        {
            Clustered = true;
        }
    }
}
```

Exercise 2

```
page 50100 "CustomerFeedbackCard"
{
    PageType = Card;
    ApplicationArea = All;
    SourceTable = "CustomerFeedback";

    layout
    {
        area(Content)
        {
            group(Group)
            {
                field("FeedbackID"; "FeedbackID")
                {
                    ApplicationArea = All;
                    Editable = false;
                }
                field("CustomerID"; "CustomerID")
                {
                    ApplicationArea = All;
                }
                field("FeedbackDate"; "FeedbackDate")
```

```
            {
                ApplicationArea = All;
            }
            field("Comments"; "Comments")
            {
                ApplicationArea = All;
            }
        }
    }
  }
}
```

CHAPTER 4

Working with Development Tools in Business Central

The chapter focuses on mastering the development tools essential for Dynamics 365 Business Central development. The chapter aims to equip readers with a comprehensive understanding of the tools and environments that form the backbone of Business Central development processes.

The chapter begins with an overview of the development tools used in Business Central. This section introduces the primary integrated development environment, Visual Studio Code, and its critical extensions for Business Central development. Coverage includes the AL programming language, which is fundamental to creating extensions and customizations in Business Central.

Following this, the chapter explores the effective utilization of development environments. This part examines how to set up and manage different types of environments using Docker containers, including sandbox, production, and local development environments. Emphasis is placed on understanding the distinctions between these environments and leveraging them for efficient development and testing.

The third section of the chapter concentrates on debugging and troubleshooting techniques. Readers will learn about various debugging tools available in Visual Studio Code as well as how to set breakpoints, step through code, and analyze variables during runtime. This section also covers common troubleshooting strategies for addressing issues in Business Central development.

Performance optimization strategies form the fourth major topic. This part discusses best practices for writing efficient AL code, optimizing database queries, and utilizing tools to identify and resolve performance bottlenecks in Business Central applications.

The chapter includes a set of practical exercises designed to reinforce the concepts covered. These hands-on activities allow readers to apply knowledge of development tools in realistic scenarios, enhancing proficiency in Business Central development.

Additionally, the chapter features case studies that illustrate real-world applications of the tools and techniques discussed. These case studies provide concrete examples of how development tools are used to solve complex problems in Business Central projects.

Overall, this chapter serves as a crucial resource for developers looking to enhance skills in using the development tools specific to Business Central, enabling the creation of more robust, efficient, and maintainable solutions.

Overview of Development Tools for Business Central

Introduction

Microsoft Dynamics 365 Business Central offers a robust set of development tools that enable developers to customize and extend the application's functionality. This section provides an overview of the primary development tools used in Business Central development.

Visual Studio Code

Visual Studio Code (VS Code) is the primary integrated development environment (IDE) for Business Central development. It offers

- Lightweight and fast performance
- Extensions for AL Language support
- Integrated debugging capabilities
- Source control integration

AL Language

AL (Application Language) is the programming language used for developing extensions in Business Central. Key features include

- Object-oriented syntax
- Direct integration with Business Central data types and structures
- Support for event-driven programming

Business Central Extension

The Business Central extension for VS Code provides

- IntelliSense and code completion for AL
- Snippets for common coding patterns
- Integration with Business Central server for publishing and testing

Azure DevOps

Azure DevOps is used for

- Source code management
- Continuous integration and continuous deployment (CI/CD)
- Work item tracking and project management

Docker

Docker containers are used to

- Create isolated development environments
- Simulate different versions of Business Central
- Facilitate testing across multiple environments

PowerShell

PowerShell scripts are utilized for

- Automating development tasks
- Managing Business Central environments
- Deploying extensions

Standalone Development Environment

Microsoft provides standalone development environments that include

- Preconfigured Business Central instance
- Sample data for testing and development
- Tools for creating and testing extensions

AL Test Runner

The AL Test Runner is a tool for

- Creating and running automated tests
- Ensuring code quality and reliability
- Integrating with CI/CD pipelines

Business Central Administration Center

This web-based tool is used for

- Managing Business Central environments
- Monitoring system health and performance
- Configuring security and user access

Utilizing Development Environments Effectively in Business Central

Introduction

Effective utilization of development environments is crucial for efficient and reliable Business Central development. This section explores various types of development environments, their purposes, and best practices for leveraging them effectively.

Types of Development Environments

1. Local Development Environment

- Setup using Docker containers
- Allows for rapid development and testing
- Provides isolation from production systems

2. Sandbox Environment

- Three Sandboxes are provisioned with each instance of Business Central.
- Cloud-based environment for testing and development.
- Mirrors production data and configurations.
- It is ideal for user acceptance testing and final quality checks.

3. Production Environment

- Live environment where the application runs
- Used for final deployment and real-world operation
- Requires careful management and controlled updates

Best Practices for Environment Management
1. Version Control

Implementing robust version control is crucial for managing Business Central development across multiple environments.

Key Points

- Use Git as the primary version control system.

- Implement a branching strategy (e.g., Gitflow) to manage feature development, releases, and hotfixes.

- Utilize feature branches for isolating work and facilitating code reviews.

- Implement pull request processes to ensure code quality before merging into main branches.

- Use tags to mark release points in the code repository.

Implementation

- Set up a centralized Git repository (e.g., Azure DevOps, GitHub) for all Business Central projects.

- Configure Git hooks to enforce commit message standards and run precommit checks.

- Integrate the version control system with your IDE (Visual Studio Code) for seamless development.

2. Continuous Integration/Continuous Deployment (CI/CD)

Implementing CI/CD pipelines ensures consistent and reliable deployments across environments.

CHAPTER 4 WORKING WITH DEVELOPMENT TOOLS IN BUSINESS CENTRAL

Key Points

- Automate build processes to compile and package AL code.
- Implement automated testing as part of the CI process.
- Use staged deployments to progressively release changes across environments.
- Implement approval gates for production deployments.

Implementation

- Utilize Azure DevOps Pipelines or GitHub Actions to create CI/CD workflows.
- Set up automatic triggers for CI pipelines on code commits or pull request creations.
- Implement automated AL unit tests and run them as part of the CI process.
- For BC on-premise hosted on Azure infrastructure, use virtual machines for deployments, and consider using Azure DevOps for staged deployments across environments.

3. Environment Parity

Maintaining similarity between development, testing, and production environments reduces environment-specific issues. This is typically managed through the Business Central Admin Center.

Key Points

- Use identical Business Central versions across all environments.

- Maintain consistent configurations across environments, especially for Business Central on-premise versions, where virtual machines are used, minimizing the impact of underlying hardware differences.

- Replicate production customizations and extensions in nonproduction environments.

Implementation

- For cloud deployments of Business Central, utilize infrastructure-as-code tools like Azure Resource Manager (ARM) templates to define and deploy consistent environments. If working with the on-premise version, equivalent tools and methods specific to your infrastructure may be used to achieve similar consistency.

- Implement a process to regularly sync configurations from production to sandbox environments.

- Use containerization (Docker) to ensure consistency in local development environments.

4. Data Management

Proper data management across environments is crucial for effective testing and development.

Key Points

- In the latest release of Business Central, data masking for sensitive information such as emails and passwords is automatically handled; these details are not replicated to sandbox environments. For older Business Central on-premise versions, ensure that data masking is manually implemented to protect sensitive information in nonproduction environments.

- Use synthetic data generation for testing specific scenarios.

- Establish a regular schedule for refreshing data in nonproduction environments.

- Perform regular backups of production data, ideally up to 10 times per month, and store these backups in Azure Blob Storage using Azure Services to ensure data integrity and recovery options.

Implementation

- Develop custom AL codeunits for data masking, focusing on personally identifiable information (PII) and financial data.

- Utilize tools like Azure Data Factory for data movement and transformation between environments.

- Implement an automated weekly process to refresh sandbox environments with masked production data.

5. Access Control

Implementing strict access policies for each environment type ensures security and compliance.

Key Points

- Follow the principle of least privilege for all environment access.

- Implement role-based access control (RBAC) for different environment types.

- Regularly audit and review access permissions.

Implementation

- Utilize Azure Active Directory for centralized identity management.

- Configure environment-specific security groups in Azure AD.

- Implement just-in-time (JIT) access for production environments.

- Set up quarterly access reviews to ensure appropriate permissions.

6. Monitoring and Logging

Comprehensive monitoring and logging across all environments aids in troubleshooting and performance optimization.

Key Points

- Implement centralized logging for all environments.
- Set up real-time monitoring for critical system metrics.
- Establish alerting mechanisms for potential issues.

Implementation

- Utilize Azure Application Insights for application-level monitoring and logging.
- Set up Azure Monitor for infrastructure and resource monitoring.
- Implement custom AL telemetry for Business Central-specific metrics.
- Configure Power BI dashboards for visualizing environment health and performance metrics.

7. Documentation

Maintaining detailed documentation of environment configurations and processes ensures consistency and facilitates knowledge transfer.

Key Points

- Document environment-specific configurations and differences.

- Maintain up-to-date deployment and operation procedures.

- Document troubleshooting guides and common issues.

Implementation

- **Use a Document Registry**: Establish a structured document registry where each document is organized with a naming convention that includes prefixes (e.g., "ENV_Config_", "DEP_Proc_") and version numbers (e.g., "v1.0", "v2.1"). This helps in ensuring that all documentation is easily traceable and accessible.

- **Version Control for Documentation**: Implement version control for documents, ensuring that changes are tracked, and previous versions are archived. This is particularly useful for maintaining the history of configurations and processes.

- **Collaborative Documentation Platform**: Use a platform like Confluence, SharePoint, or GitHub Wiki to maintain living documentation, where updates can be made collaboratively and versioning is inherently supported.

- **Documentation Review Process**: Implement a regular review process as part of the development lifecycle to ensure that all documentation is accurate and up-to-date and aligns with the current state of the environment and processes.

- **Video Tutorials and Supplementary Materials**: Create video tutorials for complex processes to supplement written documentation, making it easier for developers to understand and follow.

- **Culture of Documentation**: Foster a culture of documentation by including it in the definition of done for all development tasks, ensuring that every code change or process update is accompanied by corresponding documentation updates.

Effective Use of Docker for Local Development

1. Create custom Docker images with predefined configurations.
2. Use Docker Compose for multicontainer setups.
3. Implement volume mapping for persistent data storage.
4. Utilize Docker networks for intercontainer communication.

Sandbox Environment Strategies

1. Regular data refresh from production (with appropriate data masking)
2. Scheduled cleanup to prevent resource bloat
3. Implement a process for managing concurrent development efforts

Production Environment Considerations

1. Implement robust change management processes
2. Use feature flags for gradual rollouts
3. Establish a rollback strategy for failed deployments
4. Regular performance monitoring and optimization

Case Study: Streamlining Multienvironment Development at TechnoGlobe Inc.

Background

TechnoGlobe Inc., a medium-sized technology company, was struggling with inconsistencies between their development, testing, and production environments for their Business Central implementation. This led to frequent deployment issues and bugs that were difficult to reproduce and fix.

Challenge

The development team needed to streamline their environment management to improve code quality, reduce deployment errors, and increase overall development efficiency.

Solution

1. **Standardized Local Environments**: Implemented Docker-based local development environments for all developers, ensuring consistency across the team
2. **Automated Sandbox Refresh**: Created a scheduled process to refresh the sandbox environment with masked production data weekly

3. **CI/CD Pipeline**: Implemented an Azure DevOps pipeline for automated testing and deployment across environments

4. **Environment-Specific Configurations**: Developed a system for managing environment-specific configurations, allowing for easy switching between environments

5. **Monitoring and Logging**: Implemented centralized logging and monitoring across all environments using Azure Application Insights

Results

- Forty percent reduction in environment-related bugs
- Twenty-five percent increase in development speed
- Fifty percent decrease in time spent on deployment issues
- Improved collaboration between development and operations teams
- Enhanced trust in the system, leading to more reliable and predictable outcomes
- Increased user adoption due to smoother and more stable deployments

Key Takeaways

1. Standardized environments significantly reduce "works on my machine" issues.

2. Automated processes for environment management save time and reduce human error.

3. Proper monitoring and logging across all environments aid in quick issue resolution.

4. Investing in environment management pays off in improved code quality and developer productivity.

Debugging and Troubleshooting Techniques in Business Central

Introduction

Effective debugging and troubleshooting are crucial skills for any Business Central developer. This section covers various techniques and tools available for identifying, diagnosing, and resolving issues in Business Central applications.

1. Using the Debugger in Visual Studio Code

Visual Studio Code's debugger is a powerful tool for AL development in Business Central.

Setting Breakpoints

Breakpoints allow you to pause code execution at specific points.

- To set a breakpoint, click in the gutter (the area to the left of the line numbers) or use the F9 key.

- You can set conditional breakpoints by right-clicking on a breakpoint and selecting "Edit Breakpoint."

CHAPTER 4   WORKING WITH DEVELOPMENT TOOLS IN BUSINESS CENTRAL

Example:

```
codeunit 50100 "My Codeunit"
{
    procedure MyProcedure(var Customer: Record Customer)
    begin
        // Set a breakpoint on the next line
        Customer.Name := 'New Name'; // Breakpoint here
        Customer.Modify();
    End;
}
```

Stepping Through Code

- **Step Over (F10)**: Execute the current line and move to the next line.
- **Step Into (F11)**: Enter a method call on the current line.
- **Step Out (Shift + F11)**: Complete the execution of the current method and return to the calling method.

Watching Variables

- Use the "Watch" window to monitor specific variables.
- Hover over variables in the code to see their current values.

Using the Call Stack

The call stack shows the sequence of method calls that led to the current point of execution.

- Use it to understand the flow of your application.
- Double-click on a stack frame to navigate to that point in the code.

2. Logging and Tracing

Implementing logging in your code can greatly aid in troubleshooting issues, especially in production environments where direct debugging isn't possible.

Using AL Logging

Business Central provides built-in logging capabilities:

```
codeunit 50101 "Logging Example"
{
    procedure LogSomething()
    begin
        Log.Message('This is a log message');
        Log.Error('This is an error message');
    End;
}
```

Custom Logging

For more detailed logging, you can implement custom logging:

```
codeunit 50102 "Custom Logger"
{
    procedure LogCustomMessage(MessageText: Text; Severity:
    Option Information,Warning,Error)
    var
        LogEntry: Record "Custom Log Entry";
    begin
        LogEntry.Init();
        LogEntry."Entry No." := 0;
        LogEntry."Message Text" := MessageText;
        LogEntry.Severity := Severity;
        LogEntry."User ID" := UserId;
        LogEntry."Date and Time" := CurrentDateTime;
        LogEntry.Insert(true);
    End;
}
```

3. Error Handling

Proper error handling is crucial for creating robust applications and aiding in troubleshooting.

Try-Catch Blocks

Use try-catch blocks to handle exceptions gracefully:

```
codeunit 50103 "Error Handling Example"
{
    procedure RiskyOperation()
```

```
    var
        Customer: Record Customer;
    begin
        try
            Customer.Get('NONEXISTENT');
            // This line will not be executed if the customer
            doesn't exist
            Customer.Name := 'New Name';
            Customer.Modify();
        catch
            Error('An error occurred: %1', GetLastErrorText);
        end;
    End;
}
```

Custom Error Messages

Create meaningful error messages to aid in troubleshooting:

```
if not Customer.Get(CustomerNo) then
Error('Customer %1 does not exist. Please check the customer
number and try again.', CustomerNo);
```

4. Performance Profiling

Identifying performance bottlenecks is crucial for maintaining efficient Business Central applications.

Using the AL Profiler

The AL Profiler helps identify time-consuming operations:

Enable the AL Profiler in the launch.json file:

```
{
    "type": "al",
    "request": "launch",
    "name": "Your own server",
    "server": "http://localhost",
    "serverInstance": "BC",
    "authentication": "Windows",
    "startupObjectId": 22,
    "startupObjectType": "Page",
    "breakOnError": true,
    "launchBrowser": true,
    "enableLongRunningSqlStatements": true,
    "enableSqlInformationDebugger": true,
    "tenant": "default",
    "useProfilingFile": true
}
```

1. Run your code with the profiler enabled.
2. Analyze the resulting .alcpuprofile file to identify performance issues.

Query Performance

For database-related performance issues

1. Use the Event Viewer to identify slow-running queries.
2. Analyze query plans using SQL Server Management Studio.
3. Consider adding appropriate indexes to improve query performance.

5. Telemetry and Monitoring

Implementing telemetry can provide valuable insights into application behavior and performance in production environments.

Application Insights

Integrate Azure Application Insights for comprehensive monitoring:

1. Set up an Application Insights resource in Azure.
2. Install the Application Insights AL extension.
3. Configure the extension in your app.json:

    ```
    {
        "id": "...",
        "name": "...",
        "publisher": "...",
        "version": "...",
        "application": "...",
        "dependencies": [...],
        "idRanges": [...],
        "features": ["TranslationFile"],
        "applicationInsightsConnectionString": "YOUR_CONNECTION_STRING_HERE"
    }
    ```

4. Use the provided methods to log custom events and metrics:

    ```
    codeunit 50104 "Telemetry Example"
    {
        procedure TrackSalesOrder(SalesHeader: Record "Sales Header")
    ```

```
    begin
        Session.LogMessage('0000001',
            StrSubstNo('Sales order %1 created for
            customer %2',
            SalesHeader."No.", SalesHeader."Sell-to
            Customer No."),
            Verbosity::Normal, DataClassification::Cust
            omerContent);
    End;
}
```

Case Study: Troubleshooting a Complex Integration Issue

Background

GlobalTrade Inc., a large international trading company, implemented a custom integration between their Business Central system and an external logistics management system. After several weeks of smooth operation, users began reporting intermittent errors when processing large orders.

The Problem

Large orders occasionally failed to synchronize with the logistics system, causing discrepancies and delays. The error messages were inconsistent and provided little useful information for diagnosing the root cause.

Troubleshooting Approach

1. **Logging Enhancement**
    - Implemented detailed custom logging throughout the integration codeunit

- Logged key data points, including order numbers, sizes, and timestamps

2. **Error Handling Improvement**

    - Wrapped the main integration logic in try-catch blocks

    - Implemented more descriptive error messages, including specific error codes from the external system

3. **Performance Profiling**

    - Used the AL Profiler to identify potential bottlenecks in the integration process

    - Discovered that certain database operations were taking longer than expected for large orders

4. **Telemetry Implementation**

    - Integrated Azure Application Insights to monitor the application in real time

    - Set up custom events to track the progress of each integration attempt

5. **Debugging Sessions**

    - Conducted live debugging sessions on a copy of the production environment

    - Used breakpoints and variable watching to step through the problematic scenarios

CHAPTER 4   WORKING WITH DEVELOPMENT TOOLS IN BUSINESS CENTRAL

Root Cause

Through this comprehensive approach, the team identified two main issues:

1. A timeout occurs in the external API call for orders above a certain size.

2. A database query that was not optimized for large datasets caused excessive execution time.

3. Additionally, there were instances of missing or outdated data in the logistics system (e.g., updated destinations not being reflected in Business Central). This required implementing a quarantine mechanism for problematic data and retrying logic or reporting errors back to the API caller for resolution.

Solution

1. Implemented a chunking mechanism to break large orders into smaller, manageable pieces for the API calls

2. Optimized the database query by adding appropriate indexes and refactoring the AL code to use more efficient patterns

3. Added retry logic with exponential backoff for API calls to handle transient network issues

4. Established a quarantine process for handling missing or outdated data, with mechanisms for either retrying the operation or flagging it for manual intervention

Results

Integration failures for large orders were virtually eliminated, with a 100% success rate after implementing chunking and retry logic.

- Overall processing time for large orders improved by 60%.
- Real-time monitoring allowed for proactive issue detection and resolution, improving system reliability and user trust.

Performance Optimization Strategies in Business Central

Introduction

Performance optimization is crucial for ensuring that Business Central applications run efficiently, providing a smooth user experience and minimizing resource consumption. This section covers various strategies and techniques for optimizing performance in Business Central development.

1. Code Optimization

Efficient code is the foundation of a well-performing application. Here are key strategies for optimizing AL code:

Minimize Database Calls

Reducing the number of database calls can significantly improve performance.

- Use FindSet() instead of Find('-') when looping through records:

```
Customer.Reset();
if Customer.FindSet() then
    repeat
        // Process customer
    until Customer.Next() = 0;
```

- Use SetAutoCalcFields for frequently accessed FlowFields:

```
Customer.SetAutoCalcFields("Balance (LCY)");
if Customer.FindSet() then
    repeat
        BalanceSum += Customer."Balance (LCY)";
    until Customer.Next() = 0;
```

Optimize Loops

Efficient loop structures can greatly improve performance:

- Use FOREACH when possible, as it's generally faster than REPEAT:

```
foreach var Customer in Customer.GetView() do begin
    // Process customer
end;
```

- Avoid nested loops when possible. Consider using temporary tables or INNER JOIN queries instead.

Use Appropriate Data Types

Choosing the right data types can impact performance:

- Use Integer instead of Decimal for whole numbers.
- Use Code instead of Text for fixed-length strings.
- Use List or Dictionary for efficient in-memory operations with large datasets.

2. Query Optimization

Efficient database queries are crucial for application performance.

Use Efficient Filtering

- Apply filters as early as possible in your code.
- Use SetRange or SetFilter instead of checking conditions in AL code:

```
Customer.SetRange("No.", '10000', '20000');
Customer.SetFilter("Balance (LCY)", '>100000');
```

Leverage Keys and Indexes

- Design tables with appropriate keys and indexes.
- Use SIFT (SumIndexField Technology) for commonly used sum fields.

CHAPTER 4 WORKING WITH DEVELOPMENT TOOLS IN BUSINESS CENTRAL

Example of defining a SIFT field:

```
field(50100; "Total Sales Amount"; Decimal)
{
    FieldClass = FlowField;
    CalcFormula = Sum("Sales Line"."Amount" WHERE("Document
    Type" = FIELD("Document Type"), "Document No." = FIELD
    ("No.")));
    Editable = false;
}
```

Use Query Objects

Query objects can be more efficient for complex data retrieval:

```
query 50100 "Customer Sales"
{
    QueryType = Normal;

    elements
    {
        dataitem(Customer; Customer)
        {
            column(No; "No.")
            {
            }
            column(Name; Name)
            {
            }
            dataitem(Sales_Header; "Sales Header")
            {
                DataItemLink = "Sell-to Customer No." =
                Customer."No.";
                column(Amount; Amount)
```

```
            {
            }
            column(Order_Date; "Order Date")
            {
            }
        }
    }
  }
}
```

3. Caching Strategies

Implementing caching can significantly reduce database load and improve response times.

Implement Caching Codeunits

Create a codeunit to handle caching of frequently accessed, relatively static data:

```
codeunit 50100 "Cache Manager"
{
    var
        CustomerCache: Dictionary of [Code[20], Record
        Customer];

    procedure GetCustomer(CustomerNo: Code[20]) Customer:
    Record Customer;
    begin
        if not CustomerCache.Get(CustomerNo, Customer)
        then begin
            Customer.Get(CustomerNo);
```

```
            CustomerCache.Add(CustomerNo, Customer);
        end;
    end;

    procedure ClearCache()
    begin
        Clear(CustomerCache);
    End;
}
```

Use Temporary Tables

Temporary tables can be used for in-memory operations on large datasets:

```
var
    TempCustomer: Record Customer temporary;

procedure ProcessLargeDataset()
var
    Customer: Record Customer;
begin
    if Customer.FindSet() then
        repeat
            TempCustomer := Customer;
            TempCustomer.Insert();
        until Customer.Next() = 0;

    // Process data using TempCustomer
end;
```

4. Background Processing

Offloading time-consuming tasks to background processes can improve user experience.

Use Job Queue Entries

Job queue entries can be used for scheduled background tasks:

```
codeunit 50101 "Background Task Manager"
{
    procedure ScheduleDailyTask()
    var
        JobQueueEntry: Record "Job Queue Entry";
    begin
        JobQueueEntry.Init();
        JobQueueEntry."Object Type to Run" :=
        JobQueueEntry."Object Type to Run"::Codeunit;
        JobQueueEntry."Object ID to Run" := CODEUNIT::
        "My Daily Task";
        JobQueueEntry."Recurring Job" := true;
        JobQueueEntry.Schedule(CreateDateTime(Today, Time));
        JobQueueEntry.Insert(true);
    End;
}
```

Implement Task Scheduler

For more complex scheduling needs, implement a custom task scheduler:

```
codeunit 50102 "Task Scheduler"
{
    procedure ScheduleTask(TaskType: Option
    Daily,Weekly,Monthly; RunDateTime: DateTime)
    var
        ScheduledTask: Record "Scheduled Task";
    begin
        ScheduledTask.Init();
```

```
        ScheduledTask."Task Type" := TaskType;
        ScheduledTask."Run DateTime" := RunDateTime;
        ScheduledTask.Insert(true);
    end;

    procedure RunScheduledTasks()
    var
        ScheduledTask: Record "Scheduled Task";
    begin
        ScheduledTask.SetRange("Run DateTime", 0DT,
        CurrentDateTime);
        if ScheduledTask.FindSet() then
            repeat
                RunTask(ScheduledTask);
                ScheduledTask.Delete();
            until ScheduledTask.Next() = 0;
    end;

    local procedure RunTask(ScheduledTask: Record
    "Scheduled Task")
    begin
        case ScheduledTask."Task Type" of
            ScheduledTask."Task Type"::Daily:
                Codeunit.Run(CODEUNIT::"Daily Task");
            ScheduledTask."Task Type"::Weekly:
                Codeunit.Run(CODEUNIT::"Weekly Task");
            ScheduledTask."Task Type"::Monthly:
                Codeunit.Run(CODEUNIT::"Monthly Task");
        end;
    End;
}
```

5. Application Design Considerations

Overall application design plays a crucial role in performance.

Modularize Your Application

Break down your application into smaller, manageable modules to improve maintainability and scalability.

- **Cohesion**: Ensure that each module is highly cohesive, meaning that all the components within a module are closely related and work together towards a single purpose. This improves the clarity and focus of each module.

- **Coupling**: Aim for low coupling between modules, meaning that modules should be as independent as possible. Use events and publishers/subscribers to achieve loose coupling, allowing modules to interact without being tightly bound to each other. This flexibility makes it easier to modify or replace individual modules without impacting the entire system.

Implement Lazy Loading

Load data only when necessary:

```
page 50100 "Customer Card"
{
    // ... other page properties ...

    layout
    {
        area(Content)
```

CHAPTER 4   WORKING WITH DEVELOPMENT TOOLS IN BUSINESS CENTRAL

```
        {
            group(General)
            {
                // ... general fields ...
            }
            group(Sales)
            {
                Visible = ShowSalesInfo;
                // ... sales fields ...
            }
        }
    }

    trigger OnAfterGetRecord()
    begin
        ShowSalesInfo := false; // Initially hide sales info
    end;

    action(ShowSales)
    {
        trigger OnAction()
        begin
            ShowSalesInfo := true;
            CurrPage.Update(false);
        end;
    }

    var
        ShowSalesInfo: Boolean;
}
```

Use Page Extensions Wisely

- Avoid adding too many fields or actions to existing pages through extensions.
- Consider creating separate pages for complex functionality.

Case Study: Optimizing a Large-Scale Inventory Management System

Background

MegaRetail Corp, a multinational retail company, was experiencing significant performance issues with their Business Central-based inventory management system. The system was handling millions of SKUs across hundreds of stores, and users were reporting slow response times, especially during peak hours.

The Problem

- Inventory counts were taking hours to complete.
- Product availability checks were causing noticeable delays at point-of-sale terminals.
- Nightly batch jobs for inventory reconciliation were not completing within the allocated time window.

CHAPTER 4 WORKING WITH DEVELOPMENT TOOLS IN BUSINESS CENTRAL

Performance Optimization Approach

1. **Code Analysis and Optimization**

    - Conducted a thorough review of existing AL code.

    - Identified and refactored inefficient loops and database calls.

    - Implemented caching for frequently accessed, relatively static data like product information.

    - GitHub Copilot is an excellent tool for accomplishing this task efficiently.

2. **Database Query Optimization**

    - Analyzed and optimized key database queries using SQL Server execution plans

    - Added missing indexes on frequently queried fields

    - Implemented SIFT fields for commonly calculated sum fields

3. **Background Processing**

    - Moved noncritical operations to background job queue entries

    - Implemented a custom task scheduler for complex, periodic tasks

4. **Application Redesign**

    - Modularized the inventory management system into smaller, more manageable components

    - Implemented lazy loading for detailed product information on user interfaces

CHAPTER 4 WORKING WITH DEVELOPMENT TOOLS IN BUSINESS CENTRAL

5. **Caching Strategy**

    - Developed a multilevel caching system:
        - In-memory cache for frequently accessed data
        - Temporary tables for large dataset operations
        - Distributed cache using Redis for cross-instance data sharing

6. **Monitoring and Telemetry**

    - Implemented comprehensive telemetry using Azure Application Insights
    - Set up alerts for performance thresholds and error conditions

Implementation Highlights

1. **Efficient Stock Counting**

```
codeunit 50103 "Efficient Stock Count"
{
    procedure PerformCount(LocationCode: Code[10])
    var
        TempInventory: Record "Inventory" temporary;
        Inventory: Record Inventory;
    begin
        // Load inventory into temp table
        Inventory.SetRange("Location Code",
        LocationCode);
        if Inventory.FindSet() then
            repeat
                TempInventory := Inventory;
                TempInventory.Insert();
            until Inventory.Next() = 0;
```

```
        // Perform count operations on TempInventory
        // ...

        // Bulk update actual inventory
        if TempInventory.FindSet() then
            repeat
                Inventory := TempInventory;
                Inventory.Modify();
            until TempInventory.Next() = 0;
    End;
}
```

2. **Caching Product Information**

```
codeunit 50104 "Product Cache Manager"
{
    var
        ProductCache: Dictionary of [Code[20],
        Record Item];

    procedure GetProduct(ItemNo: Code[20])
    Item: Record Item;
    begin
        if not ProductCache.Get(ItemNo, Item)
        then begin
            Item.Get(ItemNo);
            ProductCache.Add(ItemNo, Item);
        end;
    end;

    [EventSubscriber(ObjectType::Table, Database::Item,
    'OnAfterModifyEvent', '', false, false)]
```

CHAPTER 4 WORKING WITH DEVELOPMENT TOOLS IN BUSINESS CENTRAL

```
    local procedure OnAfterModifyItem(var Rec:
    Record Item)
    begin
        if ProductCache.ContainsKey(Rec."No.") then
            ProductCache.Set(Rec."No.", Rec);
    End;
}
```

3. **Background Inventory Reconciliation**

```
codeunit 50105 "Inventory Reconciliation"
{
    procedure ScheduleReconciliation()
    var
        JobQueueEntry: Record "Job Queue Entry";
    begin
        JobQueueEntry.Init();
        JobQueueEntry."Object Type to Run" :=
        JobQueueEntry."Object Type to Run"::Codeunit;
        JobQueueEntry."Object ID to Run" :=
        CODEUNIT::"Inventory Reconciliation";
        JobQueueEntry."Earliest Start Date/Time" :=
        CreateDateTime(Today, 230000T);
        JobQueueEntry.Insert(true);
    end;

    procedure RunReconciliation()
    begin
        // Perform reconciliation in batches
        ReconcileBatch('A'..'M');
        ReconcileBatch('N'..'Z');
    end;
```

```
local procedure ReconcileBatch(ItemNoRange: Text)
var
    Item: Record Item;
begin
    Item.SetFilter("No.", ItemNoRange);
    if Item.FindSet() then
        repeat
            // Reconcile individual item
            // ...
            Commit(); // Commit after each item to
            allow parallel processing
        until Item.Next() = 0;
End;
}
```

Results

- Inventory count duration reduced by 70%.
- Product availability checks now complete in under 100ms.
- Nightly batch jobs completing within 4 hours, down from 9+ hours.
- Overall system responsiveness improved by 60%.
- User complaints about system performance reduced by 90%.

Business Central-Specific Performance Tools and Considerations for MB-820

As a Business Central developer preparing for the MB-820 certification, it's crucial to understand the platform-specific tools and considerations for performance optimization. This section covers key areas that are particularly relevant to the certification and real-world Business Central development.

1. Performance Toolkit for Microsoft Dynamics 365 Business Central

The Performance Toolkit is a set of tools and cmdlets designed to help developers and administrators diagnose and resolve performance issues in Business Central.

Key Features

- **Telemetry Collection**: Captures detailed performance data from Business Central servers
- **Performance Counters**: Monitors system resources and Business Central-specific metrics
- **Automated Testing**: Allows creation and execution of automated performance tests

Using the Performance Toolkit

1. Install the Performance Toolkit PowerShell module:

   ```
   Install-Module -Name 'Microsoft.Dynamics.Nav.Management'
   ```

2. Collect telemetry data:

   ```
   Start-NavDataCollection -ServerInstance BC
   ```

3. Analyze collected data:

   ```
   Get-NavDataCollectionSummary -ServerInstance BC
   ```

2. Database Performance Optimization

Optimizing the Business Central database is crucial for overall system performance, especially for the on-premise version, which can be hosted on Azure infrastructure.

SQL Server Query Store

The Query Store feature in SQL Server can be particularly useful for Business Central performance tuning.

Enable Query Store for your Business Central database:

```
ALTER DATABASE [YourBCDatabase]
SET QUERY_STORE = ON
(OPERATION_MODE = READ_WRITE)
```

Analyze query performance:

```
SELECT q.query_id, qt.query_text_id, qt.query_sql_text,
       p.plan_id, qrs.avg_duration
FROM sys.query_store_query_text qt
JOIN sys.query_store_query q ON qt.query_text_id = q.query_text_id
JOIN sys.query_store_plan p ON q.query_id = p.query_id
JOIN sys.query_store_runtime_stats qrs ON p.plan_id = qrs.plan_id
ORDER BY qrs.avg_duration DESC
```

Index Tuning

Use the Database Engine Tuning Advisor to optimize indexes for Business Central:

1. Generate a workload file from Business Central usage.

2. Run the Tuning Advisor:

   ```
   dta -D "YourBCDatabase" -if "WorkloadFile.sql" -of "RecommendationsOutput.sql"
   ```

3. AL Performance Best Practices

Adhering to AL-specific best practices is essential for optimal Business Central performance.

Use SetLoadFields for Partial Record Loading

When you only need specific fields from a record, use SetLoadFields to improve performance:

```
Customer.SetLoadFields("No.", Name, "Phone No.");
if Customer.FindSet() then
    repeat
        // Use only the loaded fields
    until Customer.Next() = 0;
```

Leverage OnSaveLinks for Bulk Operations

For operations involving multiple related records, use OnSaveLinks to optimize database interactions:

```
codeunit 50200 "SalesLine BatchProcessor"
```

```
{
    [EventSubscriber(ObjectType::Table, Database::"Sales Line",
    'OnSaveLinks', '', false, false)]
    local procedure OnSaveLinks(var SalesLine: Record
    "Sales Line")
    begin
        ProcessRelatedItems(SalesLine);
        UpdateInventory(SalesLine);
    end;

    local procedure ProcessRelatedItems(var SalesLine: Record
    "Sales Line")
    begin
        // Bulk processing of related items
    end;

    local procedure UpdateInventory(var SalesLine: Record
    "Sales Line")
    begin
        // Bulk inventory update
    End;
}
```

4. Cloud Performance Considerations

With Business Central's SaaS, understanding cloud-specific performance aspects is crucial.

Optimize for Azure SQL

- Use appropriate service tiers based on your workload.

- Leverage Azure SQL Database performance recommendations.
- Implement Azure SQL Database automatic tuning.

Utilize Azure Application Insights

Integrate Azure Application Insights for comprehensive performance monitoring:

1. Set up an Application Insights resource in Azure.
2. Add the Application Insights connection string to your app.json:

    ```
    {
        "id": "...",
        "name": "...",
        "publisher": "...",
        "applicationInsightsConnectionString": "InstrumentationKey=...;IngestionEndpoint=..."
    }
    ```

3. Use AL to log custom events and metrics:

    ```
    codeunit 50201 "Performance Monitoring"
    {
        procedure TrackCustomEvent(EventName: Text;
        Properties: Dictionary of [Text, Text])
        begin
            Session.LogMessage('0000001',
                EventName,
                Verbosity::Normal,
                DataClassification::SystemMetadata,
    ```

```
            TelemetryScope::ExtensionPublisher,
            Properties);
    End;
}
```

5. Performance Testing for Extensions

Implementing thorough performance testing for Business Central extensions is critical for certification and real-world success.

Create Performance Test Codeunits

Develop codeunits specifically for performance testing:

```
codeunit 50202 "Performance Test Suite"
{
    procedure RunAllTests()
    begin
        TestCustomerCreation();
        TestSalesOrderProcessing();
        TestReportGeneration();
    end;

    local procedure TestCustomerCreation()
    var
        StartTime: DateTime;
        Customer: Record Customer;
        i: Integer;
    begin
        StartTime := CurrentDateTime;
        for i := 1 to 1000 do begin
            Clear(Customer);
```

```
            Customer.Init();
            Customer.Insert(true);
        end;
        LogPerformanceResult('Customer Creation', StartTime);
    end;

    // Additional test procedures...

    local procedure LogPerformanceResult(TestName: Text;
    StartTime: DateTime)
    var
        Duration: Duration;
    begin
        Duration := CurrentDateTime - StartTime;
        Session.LogMessage('0000002',
            StrSubstNo('Performance Test: %1, Duration: %2',
            TestName, Duration),
            Verbosity::Normal,
            DataClassification::SystemMetadata,
            TelemetryScope::ExtensionPublisher,
            Dictionary of [Text, Text]);
    End;
}
```

Implement Load Testing

Use tools like Azure Load Testing to simulate real-world usage:

1. Create a load test plan in Azure Load Testing.

2. Define test scenarios that reflect typical Business Central operations.

3. Execute tests and analyze results to identify performance bottlenecks.

CHAPTER 4   WORKING WITH DEVELOPMENT TOOLS IN BUSINESS CENTRAL

Case Study: Optimizing a Complex Business Central Extension

Background

A large manufacturing company developed a custom extension for Business Central to manage their complex production processes. During the certification process for MB-820, the development team identified several performance issues that needed to be addressed.

Challenges

1. Slow loading times for production order pages
2. High CPU usage during batch job runs for material requirements planning (MRP)
3. Frequent timeouts when generating large reports

Solution Approach

1. **Code Optimization**
   - Used SetLoadFields to optimize record loading in production order pages
   - Implemented caching for frequently accessed setup data
2. **Database Optimization**
   - Analyzed query performance using SQL Server Query Store
   - Implemented new indexes based on Database Engine Tuning Advisor recommendations

3. **Background Processing**

    - Moved MRP calculations to background job queue entries

    - Implemented a custom task scheduler for large report generation

4. **Cloud Optimizations**

    - Upgraded to a higher Azure SQL Database tier to handle increased workload

    - Implemented Azure SQL Database automatic tuning

5. **Monitoring and Telemetry**

    - Integrated Azure Application Insights for comprehensive performance monitoring

    - Implemented custom telemetry for critical business processes

Implementation Highlights

1. **Optimized Production Order Page**

    ```
    page 50200 "Optimized Production Order"
    {
        SourceTable = "Production Order";

        trigger OnOpenPage()
        begin
            SetLoadFields("No.", Status, "Source Type",
                "Source No.", "Routing No.", "Inventory Posting
                            Group");
    ```

```
        end;

        // ... rest of the page definition
    }
```

2. **Background MRP Processing**

```
codeunit 50203 "MRP Processor"
{
    procedure ScheduleMRPRun()
    var
        JobQueueEntry: Record "Job Queue Entry";
    begin
        JobQueueEntry.Init();
        JobQueueEntry."Object Type to Run" :=
        JobQueueEntry."Object Type to Run"::Codeunit;
        JobQueueEntry."Object ID to Run" :=
        CODEUNIT::"MRP Processor";
        JobQueueEntry."Earliest Start Date/Time" :=
        CurrentDateTime;
        JobQueueEntry.Insert(true);
    end;

    procedure RunMRP()
    begin
        // MRP logic here
        // Use batching and commit for large datasets
    End;
}
```

CHAPTER 4   WORKING WITH DEVELOPMENT TOOLS IN BUSINESS CENTRAL

3. **Custom Telemetry for Critical Processes**

```
codeunit 50204 "Process Telemetry"
{
    procedure TrackProcessDuration(ProcessName: Text;
    StartTime: DateTime)
    var
        Duration: Duration;
        Properties: Dictionary of [Text, Text];
    begin
        Duration := CurrentDateTime - StartTime;
        Properties.Add('ProcessName', ProcessName);
        Properties.Add('Duration', Format(Duration));

        Session.LogMessage('0000003',
            StrSubstNo('Process Duration: %1',
            ProcessName),
            Verbosity::Normal,
            DataClassification::SystemMetadata,
            TelemetryScope::ExtensionPublisher,
            Properties);
    End;
}
```

Results

- Production order page loading time reduced by 65%.
- MRP processing time decreased by 40% and no longer impacts system performance during business hours.

CHAPTER 4   WORKING WITH DEVELOPMENT TOOLS IN BUSINESS CENTRAL

- Large report generation now completes successfully with 99.9% reliability.

- Overall system performance improved, meeting the requirements for MB-820 certification.

Exercise 1: Debugging and Optimizing AL Code

Objective: Debug and optimize a poorly performing AL codeunit.

Scenario: You've been given a codeunit that calculates the total sales amount for a given customer, including a loyalty discount. The code is functioning correctly but is performing poorly, especially for customers with many sales entries.

Tasks

1. Analyze the following codeunit:

```
codeunit 50100 "Sales Calculator"
{
    procedure CalculateTotalSales(CustomerNo: Code[20]): Decimal
    var
        Customer: Record Customer;
        SalesHeader: Record "Sales Header";
        SalesLine: Record "Sales Line";
        TotalAmount: Decimal;
        LoyaltyDiscount: Decimal;
    begin
        Customer.Get(CustomerNo);

        SalesHeader.SetRange("Sell-to Customer No.", CustomerNo);
        if SalesHeader.FindSet() then
```

```
            repeat
                SalesLine.SetRange("Document Type",
                SalesHeader."Document Type");
                SalesLine.SetRange("Document No.",
                SalesHeader."No.");
                if SalesLine.FindSet() then
                    repeat
                        TotalAmount +=
                        SalesLine.Amount;
                    until SalesLine.Next() = 0;
            until SalesHeader.Next() = 0;

        if Customer."Loyalty Level" = Customer."Loyalty
        Level"::Gold then
            LoyaltyDiscount := TotalAmount * 0.1
        else if Customer."Loyalty Level" =
        Customer."Loyalty Level"::Silver then
            LoyaltyDiscount := TotalAmount * 0.05;

        exit(TotalAmount - LoyaltyDiscount);
    end;
}
```

2. Identify performance issues in this code.

3. Use the debugger to step through the code and analyze its behavior.

4. Optimize the code to improve its performance.

5. Implement error handling for potential issues.

Questions

- What specific performance issues did you identify in the original code?
- How did you use the debugger to analyze the code's behavior?
- What changes did you make to optimize the code, and why?
- How did you implement error handling, and for what scenarios?

Exercise 2: Implementing Telemetry and Performance Testing

Objective: Implement telemetry and create a performance test suite for a Business Central extension.

Scenario: You've developed a new extension for managing customer orders. Now, you need to implement telemetry to monitor its performance and usage in production, as well as create a performance test suite to ensure it meets performance requirements.

Tasks

1. Implement telemetry in the following codeunit:

    ```
    codeunit 50101 "Order Manager"
    {
        procedure CreateOrder(CustomerNo: Code[20])
        var
            SalesHeader: Record "Sales Header";
        begin
            SalesHeader.Init();
    ```

```
    SalesHeader."Document Type" :=
    SalesHeader."Document Type"::Order;
    SalesHeader."No." := '';
    SalesHeader.Insert(true);
    SalesHeader.Validate("Sell-to Customer No.",
    CustomerNo);
    SalesHeader.Modify(true);
end;

procedure AddOrderLine(OrderNo: Code[20]; ItemNo:
Code[20]; Quantity: Decimal)
var
    SalesLine: Record "Sales Line";
begin
    SalesLine.Init();
    SalesLine."Document Type" :=
    SalesLine."Document Type"::Order;
    SalesLine."Document No." := OrderNo;
    SalesLine."Line No." := GetNextLineNo(OrderNo);
    SalesLine.Insert(true);
    SalesLine.Validate(Type, SalesLine.Type::Item);
    SalesLine.Validate("No.", ItemNo);
    SalesLine.Validate(Quantity, Quantity);
    SalesLine.Modify(true);
end;

local procedure GetNextLineNo(OrderNo:
Code[20]): Integer
var
    SalesLine: Record "Sales Line";
begin
```

```
        SalesLine.SetRange("Document Type",
        SalesLine."Document Type"::Order);
        SalesLine.SetRange("Document No.", OrderNo);
        if SalesLine.FindLast() then
            exit(SalesLine."Line No." + 10000);
        exit(10000);
    end;
}
```

2. Create a new codeunit for performance testing that measures the time taken to create orders with varying numbers of order lines.

3. Implement error handling and telemetry logging for critical operations.

4. Create a report to display the results of your performance tests.

Questions

- How did you implement telemetry in the Order Manager codeunit?
- What key metrics or events did you choose to log, and why?
- How did you structure your performance test suite?
- What insights can be gained from the performance test results?
- How would you use the telemetry and performance test results to improve the extension?

Solutions

Solution for Exercise 1: Debugging and Optimizing AL Code

Here's an optimized version of the Sales Calculator codeunit with improved performance, error handling, and telemetry:

```
codeunit 50100 "Sales Calculator"
{
    procedure CalculateTotalSales(CustomerNo:
    Code[20]): Decimal
    var
        Customer: Record Customer;
        SalesLine: Record "Sales Line";
        TotalAmount: Decimal;
        LoyaltyDiscount: Decimal;
        StartTime: DateTime;
        Duration: Duration;
        Dimensions: Dictionary of [Text, Text];
    begin
        StartTime := CurrentDateTime;

        if not Customer.Get(CustomerNo) then
            Error('Customer %1 not found.', CustomerNo);

        SalesLine.SetRange("Sell-to Customer No.", CustomerNo);
        SalesLine.SetFilter("Document Type", '%1|%2',
            SalesLine."Document Type"::Order,
            SalesLine."Document Type"::Invoice);
        SalesLine.CalcSums(Amount);
        TotalAmount := SalesLine.Amount;
```

```
        case Customer."Loyalty Level" of
            Customer."Loyalty Level"::Gold:
                LoyaltyDiscount := TotalAmount * 0.1;
            Customer."Loyalty Level"::Silver:
                LoyaltyDiscount := TotalAmount * 0.05;
            else
                LoyaltyDiscount := 0;
        end;

        Duration := CurrentDateTime - StartTime;
        Dimensions.Add('CustomerNo', CustomerNo);
        Dimensions.Add('Duration', Format(Duration));
        Session.LogMessage('0000001', 'Total sales calculated',
        Verbosity::Normal, DataClassification::CustomerContent,
        TelemetryScope::ExtensionPublisher, Dimensions);

        exit(TotalAmount - LoyaltyDiscount);
    end;
}
```

Explanation of changes

1. **Performance Optimization**

    - Removed nested loops by using SalesLine table directly instead of going through SalesHeader

    - Used CalcSums to calculate the total amount in a single database query

2. **Error Handling**

    - Added a check to ensure the customer exists before proceeding

3. **Code Simplification**
   - Used a case statement for loyalty discount calculation, which is more readable and maintainable

4. **Telemetry**
   - Added telemetry logging to track the duration of the calculation and the customer number

5. **Debugging**
   - To debug this code, you could set breakpoints at the beginning of the procedure and step through each line.
   - Watch the TotalAmount and LoyaltyDiscount variables to ensure they're calculated correctly.
   - Use the debugger's variable watch feature to monitor the contents of the SalesLine record after the SetRange and SetFilter operations.

Solution for Exercise 2: Implementing Telemetry and Performance Testing

Here's the Order Manager codeunit with added telemetry:

```
codeunit 50101 "Order Manager"
{
    procedure CreateOrder(CustomerNo: Code[20])
    var
        SalesHeader: Record "Sales Header";
        StartTime: DateTime;
        Duration: Duration;
```

```
        Dimensions: Dictionary of [Text, Text];
    begin
        StartTime := CurrentDateTime;

        if not Customer.Get(CustomerNo) then
            Error('Customer %1 not found.', CustomerNo);

        SalesHeader.Init();
        SalesHeader."Document Type" := SalesHeader."Document
        Type"::Order;
        SalesHeader."No." := '';
        SalesHeader.Insert(true);
        SalesHeader.Validate("Sell-to Customer No.",
        CustomerNo);
        SalesHeader.Modify(true);

        Duration := CurrentDateTime - StartTime;
        Dimensions.Add('CustomerNo', CustomerNo);
        Dimensions.Add('OrderNo', SalesHeader."No.");
        Dimensions.Add('Duration', Format(Duration));
        Session.LogMessage('0000002', 'Order created',
        Verbosity::Normal, DataClassification::CustomerContent,
        TelemetryScope::ExtensionPublisher, Dimensions);
    end;

    procedure AddOrderLine(OrderNo: Code[20]; ItemNo: Code[20];
    Quantity: Decimal)
    var
        SalesLine: Record "Sales Line";
        StartTime: DateTime;
        Duration: Duration;
        Dimensions: Dictionary of [Text, Text];
```

```
begin
    StartTime := CurrentDateTime;

    SalesLine.Init();
    SalesLine."Document Type" := SalesLine."Document
    Type"::Order;
    SalesLine."Document No." := OrderNo;
    SalesLine."Line No." := GetNextLineNo(OrderNo);
    SalesLine.Insert(true);
    SalesLine.Validate(Type, SalesLine.Type::Item);
    SalesLine.Validate("No.", ItemNo);
    SalesLine.Validate(Quantity, Quantity);
    SalesLine.Modify(true);

    Duration := CurrentDateTime - StartTime;
    Dimensions.Add('OrderNo', OrderNo);
    Dimensions.Add('ItemNo', ItemNo);
    Dimensions.Add('Quantity', Format(Quantity));
    Dimensions.Add('Duration', Format(Duration));
    Session.LogMessage('0000003', 'Order line added',
    Verbosity::Normal, DataClassification::CustomerContent,
    TelemetryScope::ExtensionPublisher, Dimensions);
end;

local procedure GetNextLineNo(OrderNo: Code[20]): Integer
var
    SalesLine: Record "Sales Line";
begin
    SalesLine.SetRange("Document Type", SalesLine."Document
    Type"::Order);
    SalesLine.SetRange("Document No.", OrderNo);
    if SalesLine.FindLast() then
        exit(SalesLine."Line No." + 10000);
```

```
        exit(10000);
    end;
}
```

Now, let's create a performance test suite:

```
codeunit 50102 "Order Performance Test"
{
    procedure RunPerformanceTests()
    var
        Customer: Record Customer;
        Item: Record Item;
        StartTime: DateTime;
        Duration: Duration;
        OrderNo: Code[20];
        i: Integer;
    begin
        if not Customer.FindFirst() then
            Error('No customers found for testing.');
        if not Item.FindFirst() then
            Error('No items found for testing.');

        // Test creating an order with 10 lines
        StartTime := CurrentDateTime;
        OrderNo := CreateTestOrder(Customer."No.",
        Item."No.", 10);
        Duration := CurrentDateTime - StartTime;
        LogTestResult('Create Order with 10 lines', Duration);

        // Test creating an order with 100 lines
        StartTime := CurrentDateTime;
        OrderNo := CreateTestOrder(Customer."No.",
        Item."No.", 100);
```

```
        Duration := CurrentDateTime - StartTime;
        LogTestResult('Create Order with 100 lines', Duration);

        // Test creating an order with 1000 lines
        StartTime := CurrentDateTime;
        OrderNo := CreateTestOrder(Customer."No.",
        Item."No.", 1000);
        Duration := CurrentDateTime - StartTime;
        LogTestResult('Create Order with 1000 lines',
        Duration);
    end;

    local procedure CreateTestOrder(CustomerNo: Code[20];
    ItemNo: Code[20]; NumberOfLines: Integer): Code[20]
    var
        OrderManager: Codeunit "Order Manager";
        OrderNo: Code[20];
        i: Integer;
    begin
        OrderManager.CreateOrder(CustomerNo);
        OrderNo := GetLastOrderNo(CustomerNo);

        for i := 1 to NumberOfLines do
            OrderManager.AddOrderLine(OrderNo, ItemNo, 1);

        exit(OrderNo);
    end;

    local procedure GetLastOrderNo(CustomerNo: Code[20]):
    Code[20]
    var
        SalesHeader: Record "Sales Header";
```

```
    begin
        SalesHeader.SetRange("Document Type",
        SalesHeader."Document Type"::Order);
        SalesHeader.SetRange("Sell-to Customer No.",
        CustomerNo);
        if SalesHeader.FindLast() then
            exit(SalesHeader."No.")
        else
            Error('No order found for customer %1',
            CustomerNo);
    end;

    local procedure LogTestResult(TestName: Text; Duration:
    Duration)
    var
        Dimensions: Dictionary of [Text, Text];
    begin
        Dimensions.Add('TestName', TestName);
        Dimensions.Add('Duration', Format(Duration));
        Session.LogMessage('0000004', 'Performance test
        result', Verbosity::Normal, DataClassification::Sy
        stemMetadata, TelemetryScope::ExtensionPublisher,
        Dimensions);
    end;
}
```

To display the results, you can create a simple report:

```
report 50100 "Performance Test Results"
{
    UsageCategory = ReportsAndAnalysis;
    ApplicationArea = All;
```

```
dataset
{
    dataitem(TestResult; "TTT-Performance Test Result")
    {
        column(TestName; "Test Name")
        { }
        column(Duration; Duration)
        { }
    }
}
requestpage
{
    layout
    {
        area(Content)
        {
            group(GroupName)
            {
                field(Name; NameSource)
                {
                    ApplicationArea = All;
                }
            }
        }
    }
}
var
    NameSource: Text;

trigger OnPreReport()
begin
```

```
        TestResult.DeleteAll();
        Codeunit.Run(Codeunit::"Order Performance Test");
    end;
}
```

> **Note** You'll need to create a table called "TTT-Performance Test Result" to store the test results. This table should have fields for "Test Name" and "Duration."

Conclusion

Throughout this chapter, we've explored the essential development tools and techniques crucial for creating efficient, robust, and high-performing solutions in Microsoft Dynamics 365 Business Central. As we conclude, let's reflect on the key points and their significance in the context of Business Central development and the MB-820 certification.

Key Takeaways

1. **Development Environment Mastery**: We've seen how setting up and effectively utilizing development environments, including local Docker containers and cloud sandboxes, is fundamental to a streamlined development process. Mastering these environments allows developers to work efficiently and test thoroughly before deploying to production.

2. **Debugging Proficiency**: The chapter emphasized the importance of debugging skills. Proficient use of Visual Studio Code's debugger, coupled with techniques like logging and error handling, enables developers to identify and resolve issues quickly, ensuring the delivery of high-quality solutions.

3. **Performance Optimization**: We delved into various strategies for optimizing AL code and database queries. Understanding and applying these techniques is crucial for creating scalable applications that perform well under real-world conditions, a key expectation for Business Central solutions.

4. **Telemetry and Monitoring**: The implementation of telemetry emerged as a critical aspect of modern Business Central development. By leveraging tools like Azure Application Insights, developers can gain valuable insights into application performance and user behavior, facilitating continuous improvement.

5. **Testing and Quality Assurance**: We explored the creation of performance test suites and the importance of comprehensive testing. These practices are essential for ensuring that extensions meet performance requirements and maintain high-quality standards.

6. **DevOps and Continuous Integration**: The chapter touched upon the integration of development tools with DevOps practices, highlighting how automated build and deployment pipelines contribute to more reliable and efficient development lifecycles.

7. **Business Central-Specific Tools:** We covered tools specific to Business Central development, such as the AL Language extension and the Business Central Performance Toolkit. Proficiency with these tools is crucial for effective development and troubleshooting in the Business Central environment.

CHAPTER 5

Integration of Business Central with Other Applications

This chapter explores the various methods and techniques for integrating Microsoft Dynamics 365 Business Central with external applications, a crucial skill for developers working with this versatile ERP system. We'll delve into five key areas of integration: Power Automate, REST services, Azure Functions, web services, and Business Central API.

The chapter begins by examining common integration scenarios and requirements, helping readers understand when and why integration is necessary in real-world business environments. We'll discuss the importance of identifying integration needs, assessing data flow requirements, and planning for scalability and performance.

Next, we'll explore various integration techniques and methods, focusing on the tools provided by Microsoft's ecosystem. This includes leveraging Power Automate for workflow automation, accessing REST services from within Business Central, utilizing Azure Functions for serverless computing, working with web services for data exchange, and harnessing the power of the Business Central API for programmatic access.

Data synchronization and consistency form a critical part of any integration strategy. We'll cover best practices for ensuring data integrity across integrated systems, handling conflicts, and maintaining real-time or near-real-time synchronization as needed. This section will also address error handling and recovery mechanisms to ensure robust integration solutions.

The chapter concludes with a comprehensive look at best practices for seamless integration. This includes tips on security considerations, performance optimization, maintainability, and documentation. We'll also discuss strategies for testing integrated systems and managing the deployment and ongoing maintenance of integration solutions.

By the end of this chapter, readers will have a solid understanding of how to integrate Dynamics 365 Business Central with external applications, equipping them with the knowledge needed to design and implement effective integration solutions in diverse business scenarios.

Comprehensive Guide to Business Central Integration Methods

1. Power Apps with Business Central

What Is Power Apps?

Power Apps is a suite of apps, services, and connectors, as well as a data platform, that provides a rapid development environment to build custom apps for your business needs. It allows users to quickly create custom business apps that connect to your business data stored either in the underlying data platform (Microsoft Dataverse) or in various online and on-premises data sources (SharePoint, Excel, Office 365, Dynamics 365, and more).

Purpose of Integration with Business Central

The integration of Power Apps with Business Central serves several key purposes:

1. **Custom User Interfaces**: Create tailored, user-friendly interfaces for specific Business Central tasks or data views.

2. **Mobile Access**: Develop mobile apps that allow users to interact with Business Central data on the go.

3. **Process Automation**: Build apps that automate specific business processes by interacting with Business Central data and functionality.

4. **Data Visualization**: Create custom dashboards and reports that pull data from Business Central.

Integration Method

Power Apps can integrate with Business Central through

- **Business Central Connector**: Use the prebuilt connector to access Business Central data and operations.

- **Custom APIs**: Leverage custom APIs created in Business Central for more specialized integrations.

2. Power Automate with Business Central

What Is Power Automate?

Power Automate (formerly Microsoft Flow) is a cloud-based service that allows users to create and automate workflows and tasks across multiple applications and services without the need for developer help.

Purpose of Integration with Business Central

Integrating Power Automate with Business Central enables

1. **Workflow Automation**: Automate business processes that span Business Central and other applications.

2. **Data Synchronization**: Keep data consistent between Business Central and other systems.

3. **Notifications and Alerts**: Set up automated notifications based on Business Central events or data changes.

4. **Approval Processes**: Implement complex approval workflows that involve Business Central data.

Integration Method

- Use the Business Central connector in Power Automate to trigger flows based on Business Central events or to perform actions in Business Central.

- Leverage HTTP requests to interact with Business Central's API for more complex scenarios.

CHAPTER 5   INTEGRATION OF BUSINESS CENTRAL WITH OTHER APPLICATIONS

3. REST Services in Business Central

What Are REST Services?

REST (Representational State Transfer) is an architectural style for designing networked applications. REST services use HTTP requests to GET, PUT, POST, and DELETE data.

Purpose of Integration

Accessing REST services from within Business Central allows

1. **External Data Retrieval**: Fetch data from external systems into Business Central.

2. **Real-Time Integration**: Enable real-time communication with external services.

3. **Extend Functionality**: Leverage external services to add features not natively available in Business Central.

Integration Method

- Use AL code to make HTTP requests to external REST endpoints.

- Implement proper authentication and error handling.

- Parse JSON responses and map data to Business Central objects.

4. Azure Functions with Business Central

What Are Azure Functions?

Azure Functions is a serverless compute service that enables you to run code on-demand without having to explicitly provision or manage infrastructure.

Purpose of Integration

Integrating Azure Functions with Business Central allows

1. **Offload Processing**: Handle complex computations or long-running tasks outside of Business Central.

2. **Scalable Operations**: Perform operations that can automatically scale based on demand.

3. **Event-Driven Architecture**: Respond to Business Central events with custom logic.

4. **Integration Hub**: Act as an intermediary between Business Central and other systems.

Integration Method

- Trigger Azure Functions from Business Central using HTTP requests.
- Use Azure Functions to call Business Central's API for bidirectional integration.
- Implement proper authentication and error handling.

5. Web Services in Business Central

What Are Web Services in Business Central?

Business Central supports both SOAP and OData web services, allowing external systems to interact with Business Central data and functionality.

Purpose of Integration

Web services in Business Central enable

1. **Data Access**: Allow external systems to read and write Business Central data.

2. **Functionality Exposure**: Expose Business Central operations for external consumption.

3. **System Integration**: Facilitate integration with a wide range of external systems.

Integration Method

- Publish page or codeunit web services in Business Central.

- Use SOAP for more complex operations or OData for RESTful data access.

- Implement proper authentication using Microsoft Entra ID.

6. Business Central API

What Is the Business Central API?

The Business Central API is a RESTful interface that provides programmatic access to Business Central data and functionality.

Purpose of Integration

The API allows

1. **Standardized Access**: Provide a consistent way to interact with Business Central data.

2. **Complex Operations**: Perform advanced operations through API endpoints.

3. **Modern Integration**: Enable integration with modern applications and services.

Integration Method

- Use HTTP requests to interact with API endpoints.
- Implement authentication using Microsoft Entra ID.
- Utilize OData query options for filtering, sorting, and pagination.

7. Shopify and Dynamics 365 Business Central (D365BC)

What Is Shopify?

Shopify is a leading e-commerce platform that allows businesses to create and manage their online stores. It provides a range of tools for managing products, orders, and customer interactions.

Purpose of Integration with D365BC

Integrating Shopify with D365BC offers several key benefits:

- **Seamless Data Synchronization**: Automatically sync orders, customers, and inventory data between Shopify and D365BC.

- **Streamlined Operations**: Improve efficiency by automating data transfer and reducing manual data entry.

- **Enhanced Reporting**: Combine e-commerce and financial data for comprehensive reporting and analysis.

Integration Method

Shopify provides a standard connector to D365BC with the following features:

- **Prebuilt Connector**: Utilize the out-of-the-box connector for seamless integration, which includes all required functionalities such as data synchronization and order management.

- **No Custom Development Required**: The standard connector covers most use cases, eliminating the need for custom extensions, MDMs, or Azure Functions.

8. Power Pages

What Are Power Pages?

Power Pages, formerly known as Power Apps Portals, are a component of the Power Apps suite that allows you to create and manage external-facing websites. These websites can be used to extend the functionality of Dynamics 365 Business Central (D365BC) by providing self-service portals for customers, vendors, and other stakeholders.

Purpose of Power Pages with D365BC

The use of Power Pages with D365BC provides several advantages:

- **Customer and Vendor Portals**: Create custom portals where customers and vendors can view and interact with their data stored in D365BC.

- **Enhanced User Experience**: Provide a user-friendly interface for external users to access business information and services.

- **Extended Functionality**: Allow for custom functionality and data interactions beyond the standard D365BC interface.

Integration Method

Power Pages integrate with D365BC through

- **Prebuilt Templates**: Use out-of-the-box templates to quickly set up customer or vendor portals.

- **Custom Configuration**: Tailor the portals to meet specific business needs using the built-in customization options.

Understanding Integration Scenarios and Requirements for Business Central

Introduction

Integrating Business Central with other systems is crucial for many organizations to streamline their operations and enhance data flow across different business processes. Understanding various integration scenarios and their requirements is the first step in implementing successful integrations.

Common Integration Scenarios

1. **E-commerce Integration**: Connecting Business Central with an e-commerce platform to synchronize inventory, orders, and customer data

2. **CRM Integration**: Linking Business Central with a customer relationship management system to maintain consistent customer information and sales data

3. **Supply Chain Management**: Integrating with supplier systems for automated purchase order processing and inventory updates

4. **Banking and Financial Services**: Connecting with banking systems for automated reconciliation and payment processing

5. **Business Intelligence and Reporting**: Integrating with BI tools to provide comprehensive data analysis and reporting capabilities

6. **Human Resources Management**: Linking with HR systems to synchronize employee data and payroll information

Key Requirements for Integration

1. **Data Mapping**: Identifying corresponding data fields between Business Central and the external system

2. **Real-Time vs. Batch Processing**: Determining whether data needs to be synchronized in real time or can be processed in batches

3. **Error Handling and Logging**: Implementing robust error handling and logging mechanisms to manage integration failures

4. **Security and Compliance**: Ensuring data security and compliance with relevant regulations (e.g., GDPR, CCPA)

5. **Scalability**: Designing the integration to handle growing data volumes and increased transaction frequencies

6. **Performance Optimization**: Minimizing the impact on system performance, especially for real-time integrations

7. **User Authentication and Authorization**: Managing user access and permissions across integrated systems

8. **Data Validation and Integrity**: Implementing checks to maintain data quality and consistency across systems

Detailed Case Study: E-commerce Integration for Worldwide Traders

Company Background

Worldwide Traders is a medium-sized retail company specializing in outdoor gear and equipment. Founded in 2005, the company has grown from a single brick-and-mortar store to a regional chain with 15 locations across the northwestern United States. Their product range includes camping equipment, hiking gear, outdoor clothing, and accessories.

Current System Landscape

- **ERP**: Microsoft Dynamics 365 Business Central (on-premises deployment)
- **POS**: Integrated Business Central POS module
- **Inventory Management**: Managed through Business Central
- **Customer Management**: Basic customer data stored in Business Central

CHAPTER 5 INTEGRATION OF BUSINESS CENTRAL WITH OTHER APPLICATIONS

Business Challenge

With the growing trend in online shopping, Worldwide Traders realized they were missing out on a significant market segment. They decided to launch an e-commerce website to reach a broader customer base and compete with larger online retailers. However, they faced the challenge of integrating their new online store with their existing Business Central system to ensure seamless operations.

Integration Scenario: Business Central and Shopify Integration

Project Objectives

1. Launch a fully functional e-commerce website using Shopify
2. Integrate Shopify with Business Central for seamless data flow
3. Maintain real-time inventory accuracy across online and offline channels
4. Streamline order processing and fulfillment
5. Provide a unified customer experience across all sales channels

Detailed Integration Requirements

1. Inventory Synchronization

- Real-time updates of stock levels from Business Central to Shopify

CHAPTER 5   INTEGRATION OF BUSINESS CENTRAL WITH OTHER APPLICATIONS

- o   Implement bidirectional sync to update stock levels every 5 minutes
- o   Set up alerts for items with stock levels below 20% of par level
- Handle multilocation inventory
  - o   Aggregate stock levels from all physical stores and warehouses
  - o   Implement logic to allocate online orders to specific locations based on inventory availability and shipping address

2. Order Management

- Automatic creation of sales orders in Business Central for online purchases.
  - o   Create a new sales order in Business Central within 2 minutes of order placement on Shopify.
  - o   Map Shopify order fields to corresponding Business Central fields (e.g., customer info, line items, totals).
- Real-time order status updates from Business Central to Shopify
  - o   Update order status in Shopify when changed in Business Central (e.g., processing, shipped, delivered).
  - o   Implement status mapping between Business Central and Shopify (e.g., "Released" in BC = "Processing" in Shopify).

3. Customer Data

- Bidirectional synchronization of customer information
  - Create new customer records in Business Central for new Shopify customers.
  - Update existing customer information in both systems when changes occur.
- Consolidation of customer purchase history across online and offline channels
  - Implement a unified customer view in Business Central, showing both online and in-store purchases.
  - Create a mechanism to match and merge customer records from different channels.

4. Product Information

- Syncing of product details, pricing, and images from Business Central to Shopify
  - Set up initial bulk product upload from Business Central to Shopify.
  - Implement ongoing sync for product updates (e.g., price changes, new products, discontinued items).
- Management of product categories and attributes
  - Map Business Central item categories to Shopify collections.
  - Sync custom attributes (e.g., brand, material, size) from Business Central to Shopify product metadata.

5. Financial Reconciliation

- Daily synchronization of sales transactions for accounting purposes
    - Create a daily summary of online sales in Business Central.
    - Reconcile Shopify payments with bank deposits.
- Automated reconciliation of online payments with bank statements
    - Integrate with payment gateway to match transactions.
    - Handle refunds and chargebacks consistently across both systems.

Integration Solution Architecture

To meet the integration requirements, Worldwide Traders implemented the following solution for a lesser-known shopping cart platform without a standard connector:

1. **Use of Business Central API**
    - **OData API Utilization**: Leveraged Business Central's OData API for real-time data exchange with the shopping cart platform
    - **Custom API Endpoints**: Developed custom API endpoints to handle specific business logic, such as complex inventory allocation

2. **Power Automate Flows**
   - **Inventory Update Flow**
     - **Trigger**: Activated every 5 minutes or upon changes in stock levels in Business Central
     - **Action**: Updates product inventory in the shopping cart platform
   - **New Order Processing Flow**
     - **Trigger**: Initiated when a new order is created in the shopping cart platform
     - **Actions**
       - Creates a sales order in Business Central
       - Allocates inventory
       - Updates order status in the shopping cart platform
   - **Customer Data Sync Flow**
     - **Trigger**: Activated when customer data changes in either Business Central or the shopping cart platform
     - **Action**: Synchronizes customer data between Business Central and the shopping cart platform
3. **Azure Functions**
   - **Inventory Aggregation Function**
     - Aggregates inventory data from multiple locations
     - Runs every 5 minutes to update available-to-promise inventory

- **Data Transformation Function**
  - Handles complex data mappings between Business Central and the shopping cart platform
  - Processes bulk data updates, such as initial product catalog uploads

4. **Webhooks for Real-Time Updates**
   - Set up webhooks in the shopping cart platform to trigger updates in Business Central for
     - New orders
     - Order cancellations
     - Customer registrations and updates
     - Product updates for two-way sync scenarios

5. **Error Handling and Monitoring**
   - **Monitoring and Logging**: Implemented Azure Application Insights for comprehensive monitoring and logging
   - **Error Handling Framework**
     - Logs errors in Azure Blob Storage
     - Sends alerts for critical errors via email and SMS
   - **Real-Time Monitoring**: Developed a Power BI dashboard to monitor integration processes in real time

CHAPTER 5   INTEGRATION OF BUSINESS CENTRAL WITH OTHER APPLICATIONS

Implementation Process

- **Discovery and Planning (2 Weeks)**
    - Detailed requirements gathering
    - System analysis of both Business Central and the shopping cart platform
    - Integration architecture design
- **Development (8 Weeks)**
    - Set up development environments
    - Develop and test individual integration components
    - Implement error handling and monitoring solutions
- **Testing (3 Weeks)**
    - Unit testing of individual components
    - Integration testing of the entire system
    - Performance testing, especially for real-time synchronization
    - User acceptance testing with key stakeholders
- **Deployment (1 Week)**
    - Set up production environments
    - Migrate initial data (products, customers)
    - Go live with parallel run of old and new systems

- **Post Implementation (4 Weeks)**
  - Monitoring and fine-tuning
  - User training and support
  - Documentation and knowledge transfer

Challenges Faced and Solutions

1. **Performance Issues with Real-Time Sync**
   - **Challenge**: Initial real-time sync caused performance degradation in Business Central during high-traffic periods
   - **Solution**: Implemented a queuing system using Azure Service Bus to manage high volumes of updates without overloading Business Central

2. **Complex Product Variations**
   - **Challenge**: Handling products with multiple variants (size, color, etc.) differently in Business Central and Shopify
   - **Solution**: Developed a custom mapping logic in Azure Functions to translate between Business Central's item variants and Shopify's product options

3. **Data Inconsistencies**
   - **Challenge**: Occasional data mismatches between systems due to failed syncs or manual overrides
   - **Solution**: Implemented a daily reconciliation process and developed a UI for manual resolution of discrepancies

Outcomes and Benefits

After six months of operation with the new integrated system, Worldwide Traders experienced

1. **Increased Sales**
   - Thirty percent increase in overall sales, with online sales accounting for 25% of total revenue
   - Fifteen percent increase in in-store sales due to "click and collect" functionality

2. **Improved Operational Efficiency**
   - Fifty percent reduction in order processing time
   - Seventy percent decrease in inventory discrepancies between online and in-store
   - Forty percent reduction in customer service calls related to order status inquiries

3. **Enhanced Customer Experience**
   - Twenty-five percent increase in customer satisfaction scores
   - Twenty percent increase in repeat customer rate

4. **Better Business Insights**
   - Real-time visibility into sales and inventory across all channels
   - Improved forecast accuracy, leading to 18% reduction in stockouts

Lessons Learned

1. **Importance of Real-time Synchronization**: Real-time inventory updates were crucial in preventing overselling and improving customer satisfaction. However, the implementation required careful performance tuning.

2. **Data Mapping Complexity**: The project revealed unexpected complexities in mapping data between systems, particularly for product variants and customer information. Early and thorough data analysis is crucial.

3. **Scalability Planning**: The initial integration design needed adjustments to handle peak season traffic, emphasizing the importance of scalability in the initial planning. Load testing with projected peak volumes is essential.

4. **User Training**: Comprehensive training for staff on the integrated systems was vital for successful adoption and operation. This included not just software training but also new business process training.

5. **Continuous Monitoring and Optimization**: Post implementation, continuous monitoring and periodic reviews were necessary to optimize the integration, especially as business needs evolved.

6. **Change Management**: The project's success heavily depended on effective change management, including clear communication with all stakeholders and phased implementation of new features.

Integration Techniques and Methods for Dynamics 365 Business Central

Introduction

Integrating Microsoft Dynamics 365 Business Central with other systems and applications is crucial for creating a cohesive and efficient business ecosystem. This document outlines various integration techniques and methods available for Business Central, their use cases, advantages, and considerations.

1. APIs (Application Programming Interfaces)

Description

Business Central provides a rich set of APIs that allow external systems to interact with its data and functionality.

Techniques

- **OData REST APIs**: Standard REST APIs following the OData protocol
- **Custom APIs**: Developer-created APIs for specific business needs

Use Cases

- Real-time data exchange with external systems
- Mobile app integration
- Custom front-end development

Advantages

- Standard, well-documented interfaces
- Supports real-time integration
- Scalable and performance-efficient
- Security/authentication

Considerations

- Requires developer expertise
- Need to manage authentication and authorization
- Rate limiting and performance optimization

2. Web Services

Description

Business Central supports both SOAP and OData web services, allowing external systems to consume BC functionality.

Techniques

- **Page Web Services**: Expose data from specific pages
- **Codeunit Web Services**: Expose functionality (methods) from codeunits

Use Cases

- Integration with legacy systems
- Complex data operations
- Exposing specific business logic

Advantages

- Can expose complex business logic
- Supports both SOAP and REST protocols
- Familiarity for developers experienced with earlier NAV versions

Considerations

- More complex to set up compared to standard APIs
- May require more maintenance as BC evolves
- Performance can be an issue for large datasets

3. Power Automate (Microsoft Flow)

Description

A cloud-based service that allows creation of workflows across multiple applications and services.

Techniques

- **Triggers**: Start flows based on events in Business Central
- **Actions**: Perform operations in Business Central or other systems
- **Connectors**: Prebuilt integrations with many popular services

Use Cases

- Automating business processes across multiple systems
- Notifications and alerts
- Simple data synchronization tasks

Advantages

- Low-code/no-code solution
- Wide range of prebuilt connectors
- Easy to set up and modify

Considerations

- Limited for complex business logic
- Can become costly with high-volume transactions
- Governance and management of flows in large organizations

4. Power Apps

Description

A suite of apps, services, and connectors that provides a rapid development environment for building custom apps.

Techniques

- **Canvas Apps**: Create custom UIs that interact with Business Central data
- **Model-driven Apps**: Build complex forms and views based on Business Central data

Use Cases

- Custom mobile apps for specific business processes
- Employee self-service portals
- Customer or vendor portals

Advantages

- Rapid development of custom UIs
- Integration with other Microsoft services
- Supports both web and mobile platforms

Considerations

- Learning curve for complex apps
- Licensing costs for Power Apps
- Performance considerations for large datasets

5. Azure Functions

Description

Serverless compute service that enables running code on-demand without managing infrastructure.

Techniques

- **HTTP Triggers**: Run code in response to HTTP requests
- **Timer Triggers**: Execute code on a schedule
- **Queue Triggers**: Process Business Central data in response to messages in a queue

Use Cases

- Complex data transformations
- Scheduled data synchronization
- Offloading resource-intensive operations from Business Central

Advantages

- Highly scalable
- Pay-per-execution pricing model
- Can be written in multiple programming languages

Considerations

- Requires Azure subscription and management
- Cold start times for infrequently used functions
- Monitoring and error handling complexity

6. Event-Driven Architecture

Description

Utilize Business Central's built-in events or custom events to trigger integrations.

Techniques

- **Business Events**: Predefined events in Business Central
- **Integration Events**: Custom events created by developers
- **Event Subscribers**: Code that runs in response to specific events

Use Cases

- Real-time synchronization with external systems
- Audit trailing
- Triggering external processes based on Business Central actions

Advantages

- Enables loose coupling between systems
- Supports real-time integrations
- Can significantly reduce polling and improve performance

Considerations

- Requires careful design to avoid performance issues
- Need to handle failed event processing and retries
- Can increase complexity of the overall system

7. Batch Processing

Description

Periodic processing of data in bulk between Business Central and external systems.

Techniques

- **Scheduled Jobs**: Use BC's job queue to run integration tasks
- **ETL Tools**: Utilize Extract, Transform, Load tools for data movement
- **Import/Export Functionality**: Use BC's built-in data import/export features

Use Cases

- Nightly synchronization of large datasets
- Periodic financial reconciliations
- Bulk updates from external systems

Advantages

- Efficient for large volumes of data
- Reduces real-time processing load
- Simpler to implement and troubleshoot

Considerations

- Data may not be immediately consistent across systems
- Need to handle failures and restarts for long-running jobs
- May require significant processing windows

Data Synchronization and Consistency in Business Central Integrations

Introduction

Maintaining data synchronization and consistency is crucial when integrating Microsoft Dynamics 365 Business Central with other systems. This ensures that all connected systems have accurate, up-to-date information, which is vital for making informed business decisions and maintaining operational efficiency.

Key Concepts

1. Data Synchronization

Data synchronization is the process of maintaining data consistency across multiple systems by ensuring that changes made in one system are reflected in all other connected systems.

2. Data Consistency

Data consistency refers to the accuracy and validity of data across all integrated systems. It ensures that the same data has the same value regardless of where it is accessed.

Synchronization Methods

1. Real-Time Synchronization

- **Description**: Data is updated across systems immediately when changes occur.
- **Techniques**
    - Webhooks
    - API calls triggered by events
    - Message queues with immediate processing
- **Advantages**
    - Provides up-to-the-minute data accuracy
    - Ideal for critical business processes requiring immediate updates

- **Challenges**
    - Can increase system load and complexity
    - Requires robust error handling and retry mechanisms

2. Batch Synchronization

- **Description**: Data updates are collected and processed at scheduled intervals.
- **Techniques**
    - Scheduled jobs in Business Central
    - ETL (Extract, Transform, Load) processes
    - Periodic API calls or data exports/imports
- **Advantages**
    - More efficient for large volumes of data
    - Reduces system load during peak business hours
- **Challenges**
    - Data may not be immediately consistent across systems
    - Requires careful scheduling to balance timeliness and system performance

3. Hybrid Approach

- **Description**: Combines real-time and batch synchronization methods

CHAPTER 5   INTEGRATION OF BUSINESS CENTRAL WITH OTHER APPLICATIONS

- **Technique**: Use real-time sync for critical data and batch for less time-sensitive information
- **Advantages**
    - Balances system performance with data timeliness
    - Provides flexibility to handle different data types and volumes
- **Challenges**
    - Increased complexity in design and implementation
    - Requires clear rules for determining which data uses which sync method

Ensuring Data Consistency

1. Master Data Management (MDM)

- Focuses on ensuring master data consistency between companies within the same organization, particularly subsidiaries
- Supports synchronization of key data entities (e.g., customers, products) between Business Central and Microsoft Dataverse
- Does not natively support synchronization with external data sources like MS SQL Server or other data storage platforms beyond Dataverse
- Use unique identifiers to link records across systems, primarily within the Business Central environment and Dataverse

2. Data Validation and Cleansing

- Implement data validation rules in Business Central and integrated systems.
- Use data cleansing processes to correct and standardize data before synchronization.
- Regularly audit data quality and consistency across systems.

3. Conflict Resolution

- Develop clear rules for handling conflicting updates (e.g., last-write-wins, manual resolution).
- Implement logging and notification systems for conflict detection.
- Create processes for manual review and resolution of complex conflicts.

4. Version Control and Historization

- Maintain version history of important data changes.
- Implement audit trails to track data modifications across systems.
- Consider using temporal tables in SQL Server for historical data tracking.

Handling Synchronization Failures

1. Error Logging and Monitoring

- Implement comprehensive error logging for all synchronization processes.
- Set up monitoring and alerting systems to detect synchronization failures.
- Use tools like Azure Application Insights for real-time monitoring and diagnostics.

2. Retry Mechanisms

- Implement intelligent retry logic for failed synchronizations.
- Use exponential backoff strategies to avoid overwhelming systems during issues.
- Consider using Azure Service Bus or similar message queuing services for reliable message delivery.

3. Manual Intervention Processes

- Develop tools and processes for manual data reconciliation when needed.
- Create clear escalation procedures for addressing persistent synchronization issues.
- Train support staff on troubleshooting and resolving common sync problems.

Best Practices for Data Synchronization and Consistency

1. **Design for Idempotency**: Ensure that synchronization operations can be safely retried without causing data duplication or corruption.

2. **Use Transactional Processing**: Implement transactional processing where possible to ensure data integrity during complex updates.

3. **Implement Change Tracking**: Utilize change tracking features in Business Central and other systems to efficiently identify and synchronize only changed data.

4. **Optimize Data Models**: Design data models that are conducive to efficient synchronization, considering factors like normalization and denormalization.

5. **Manage Reference Data**: Ensure consistent handling of reference data (e.g., status codes, country lists) across all integrated systems.

6. **Regular Reconciliation**: Schedule periodic full data reconciliations to catch and correct any inconsistencies that may have been missed.

7. **Performance Tuning**: Regularly monitor and optimize synchronization processes for performance, especially as data volumes grow.

8. **Documentation**: Maintain clear documentation of data flows, synchronization rules, and conflict resolution procedures.

Case Study: Implementing Robust Data Synchronization

Scenario

A retail company integrates Business Central with an e-com platform with no standard connector to BC and A CRM system with no standard connector to BC.

Challenge

Ensuring consistent customer, inventory, and order data across all three systems.

Solution

1. **Master Data Management**

    - Establish Business Central as the master for product data.
    - Use the CRM as the master for customer data.
    - Implement bidirectional sync with clear update rules.

2. **Synchronization Strategy**

    - Real-time sync for orders and inventory updates
    - Batch sync for customer data updates (nightly)
    - Near real-time sync for product data changes (every 15 minutes)

3. **Conflict Resolution**
    - Implement a "last-write-wins" strategy with a central timestamp server.
    - Flag conflicts for manual review when automatic resolution is not possible.
4. **Error Handling**
    - Implement a centralized error queue using Azure Service Bus.
    - Develop a custom dashboard for monitoring and managing sync errors.

Outcome

- 99.9% data consistency achieved across all systems
- Significant reduction in manual data entry and reconciliation efforts
- Improved customer satisfaction due to consistent information across all touchpoints

Best Practices for Seamless Integration with Dynamics 365 Business Central

1. Thorough Planning and Analysis

1.1 Requirements Gathering

- Conduct comprehensive stakeholder interviews.

CHAPTER 5   INTEGRATION OF BUSINESS CENTRAL WITH OTHER APPLICATIONS

- Document all integration touchpoints and data flows.
- Clearly define the scope and objectives of the integration.

1.2 System Analysis

- Analyze the data structures and business logic of all systems involved.
- Identify potential data conflicts or inconsistencies.
- Assess the volume and frequency of data exchanges.

1.3 Integration Strategy

- Choose appropriate integration methods based on requirements (e.g., real-time vs. batch).
- Define clear data ownership and master data management strategies.
- Plan for scalability and future expansion.

2. Robust Architecture Design

2.1 Loose Coupling

- Design integrations with minimal dependencies between systems.
- Use intermediate data formats (e.g., JSON, XML) for data exchange.

- Implement message queues for asynchronous communication.

2.2 Scalability

- Design for horizontal scalability to handle increased loads.
- Use cloud services (e.g., Azure Functions) for elastic scaling.
- Implement caching mechanisms where appropriate.

2.3 Error Handling and Resilience

- Implement comprehensive error logging and monitoring.
- Design retry mechanisms with exponential backoff.
- Use circuit breakers to prevent cascade failures.

3. Efficient Data Management

3.1 Data Mapping and Transformation

- Create detailed data mapping documents.
- Implement data validation at both source and destination.
- Use ETL tools or custom logic for complex data transformations.

3.2 Incremental Synchronization

- Implement change data capture (CDC) mechanisms.
- Use delta synchronization to minimize data transfer.
- Optimize large data transfers with batching and pagination.

3.3 Data Consistency

- Implement transactional processing for critical operations.
- Use idempotent operations to prevent data duplication.
- Regularly reconcile data between systems to catch discrepancies.

4. Security and Compliance

4.1 Authentication and Authorization

- Use OAuth 2.0 or OpenID Connect for secure authentication.
- Implement proper role-based access control (RBAC).
- Regularly rotate API keys and secrets.

4.2 Data Protection

- Encrypt data in transit using TLS/SSL.
- Implement data masking for sensitive information.

- Ensure compliance with relevant regulations (e.g., GDPR, CCPA).

4.3 Audit Trails

- Implement comprehensive logging of all integration activities.
- Maintain audit trails for data modifications.
- Regularly review logs for security anomalies.

5. Performance Optimization

5.1 Efficient API Usage

- Minimize API calls through batching and caching.
- Implement pagination for large datasets.
- Use compression for data transfers

5.2 Asynchronous Processing

- Use asynchronous operations for noncritical, time-consuming tasks.
- Implement webhooks for event-driven integrations.
- Utilize message queues for load leveling.

5.3 Caching

- Implement caching for frequently accessed, rarely changing data.

CHAPTER 5   INTEGRATION OF BUSINESS CENTRAL WITH OTHER APPLICATIONS

- Use distributed caching solutions for scalability.
- Implement cache invalidation strategies to maintain data freshness.

6. Testing and Quality Assurance

6.1 Comprehensive Testing

- Develop a thorough test plan covering all integration scenarios.
- Implement automated integration tests.
- Conduct performance and load testing under realistic conditions.

6.2 Staging Environment

- Maintain a staging environment that mirrors production.
- Perform integration testing in the staging environment before deployment.
- Use production-like data volumes in staging for accurate testing.

6.3 Monitoring and Alerting

- Implement real-time monitoring of integration points.
- Set up alerts for critical errors and performance issues.
- Use application performance monitoring (APM) tools for deep insights.

7. Documentation and Knowledge Management

7.1 Integration Documentation

- Maintain up-to-date documentation of all integration points.
- Document data flows, transformations, and business rules.
- Keep a record of all configuration settings and environment details.

7.2 Change Management

- Implement a robust change management process.
- Maintain version control for all integration code and configurations.
- Communicate changes to all relevant stakeholders.

7.3 Knowledge Transfer

- Conduct regular knowledge sharing sessions.
- Create and maintain user guides and troubleshooting documentation.
- Implement a system for capturing and sharing lessons learned.

8. Continuous Improvement

8.1 Performance Monitoring

- Regularly review integration performance metrics.
- Identify and address bottlenecks.
- Continuously optimize based on real-world usage patterns.

8.2 User Feedback

- Establish channels for user feedback on the integrated systems.
- Regularly survey stakeholders for improvement suggestions.
- Prioritize and implement high-impact improvements.

8.3 Stay Updated

- Keep abreast of new features and updates in Business Central.
- Regularly assess new integration technologies and methods.
- Plan for periodic reviews and upgrades of the integration solution.

9. Governance and Support

9.1 Integration Governance

- Establish an integration governance committee.
- Define clear roles and responsibilities for managing integrations.
- Implement policies for integration development and management.

9.2 Support Structure

- Set up a dedicated support team for integration issues.
- Establish clear escalation procedures.
- Implement a ticketing system for tracking and resolving integration-related issues.

9.3 SLAs and Metrics

- Define clear Service Level Agreements (SLAs) for integration performance.
- Establish key performance indicators (KPIs) for measuring integration success.
- Regularly review and report on integration metrics.

CHAPTER 5 INTEGRATION OF BUSINESS CENTRAL WITH OTHER APPLICATIONS

Checklist for Business Central: E-commerce Integration Design

1. Integration Method Selection

- Chosen appropriate integration method(s)
- Justified the selection of integration method(s)
- Considered real-time vs. batch processing needs
- Evaluated scalability requirements

2. Architecture Design

- Created a high-level architecture diagram
- Identified all major components of the integration
- Defined data flow between systems
- Considered error handling and retry mechanisms
- Included message queuing for reliable communication
- Addressed scalability in the architecture

3. Data Synchronization Strategy

3.1 Product Information

- Planned initial bulk sync method
- Defined strategy for ongoing product updates
- Addressed inventory level synchronization
- Considered product variant handling

3.2 Order Management

- Designed process for importing orders from Shopify to BC
- Planned order status update mechanism from BC to Shopify
- Addressed order cancellation and refund scenarios

3.3 Customer Information

- Defined bidirectional customer sync strategy
- Addressed handling of guest checkouts
- Planned for customer data privacy and compliance

3.4 Inventory Updates

- Designed near real-time inventory update mechanism
- Addressed multilocation inventory if applicable
- Planned for handling of backordered items

4. Security Considerations

- Planned for secure API authentication
- Addressed data encryption in transit
- Considered data access controls and auditing

5. Performance Optimization

- Identified potential performance bottlenecks
- Planned caching strategies where appropriate
- Considered batch processing for bulk operations

6. Error Handling and Monitoring

- Designed comprehensive error logging mechanism
- Planned for monitoring and alerting system
- Defined strategy for handling failed transactions

7. Data Validation and Integrity

- Planned data validation checks
- Designed conflict resolution strategies
- Considered data reconciliation process

8. Testing Strategy

- Outlined plan for unit testing
- Defined approach for integration testing
- Planned for performance and load testing

9. Deployment and Maintenance

- Considered staged rollout strategy
- Planned for data migration if needed
- Defined ongoing maintenance and update procedures

10. Documentation and Training

- Planned for creation of technical documentation
- Outlined user training requirements
- Considered creation of troubleshooting guides

11. Compliance and Legal Considerations

- Addressed relevant data protection regulations (e.g., GDPR)
- Considered contractual obligations with Shopify
- Planned for data retention and deletion policies

12. Future-proofing

- Considered potential future enhancements
- Planned for versioning of integration components
- Addressed potential scalability needs

13. Best Practices Implementation

- Identified at least three best practices to implement
- Justified the selection of these best practices
- Outlined how these practices will be incorporated

Conclusion

The integration of Microsoft Dynamics 365 Business Central with other applications stands as a cornerstone of modern business process optimization. Throughout this chapter, we've traversed the complex landscape of integration scenarios, techniques, data management strategies, and best practices. This journey underscores the critical role that effective integration plays in leveraging the full potential of Business Central within a broader ecosystem of business applications.

Our exploration began with the crucial step of understanding integration scenarios and requirements. This foundation emphasized the importance of aligning technical solutions with business objectives, a theme that resonated throughout the chapter. By thoroughly analyzing business needs and technical constraints before embarking on integration projects, developers and architects can ensure that their solutions deliver tangible value and address real-world challenges.

The diverse array of integration techniques and methods discussed highlights the flexibility and adaptability of Business Central. From RESTful APIs and web services to low-code solutions, like Power Automate and Power Apps, and cloud-native options such as Azure Functions, the platform offers a rich toolkit for crafting integrations. This versatility enables developers to choose the most appropriate approach based on specific use cases, existing infrastructure, and desired outcomes.

CHAPTER 5   INTEGRATION OF BUSINESS CENTRAL WITH OTHER APPLICATIONS

The ability to leverage these various methods positions Business Central as a central hub in complex, interconnected business environments.

Data synchronization and consistency emerged as critical challenges in integration projects. The strategies outlined for managing real-time and batch synchronization, resolving conflicts, and maintaining data integrity across systems are essential for ensuring the reliability of integrated solutions. These practices not only safeguard the accuracy of business data but also build trust in the integrated systems among users and stakeholders.

The best practices for seamless integration encompassed a wide range of considerations, from robust architecture design and efficient data management to security, performance optimization, and ongoing maintenance. These guidelines serve as a roadmap for creating integrations that are not only functional but also secure, scalable, and maintainable. By adhering to these best practices, developers can significantly enhance the success rate of their integration projects and ensure the long-term viability of their solutions.

As we conclude, it's crucial to recognize that integration is an ongoing journey rather than a destination. The rapidly evolving business and technology landscapes demand that integration solutions remain agile and adaptable. Developers and architects must stay informed about emerging technologies and methodologies to continually refine and enhance their integration strategies. The future of Business Central integration holds exciting possibilities, with technologies like AI and machine learning poised to enable more intelligent and predictive integrations.

In the context of the MB-820 Microsoft Dynamics 365 Business Central Developer certification, the concepts covered in this chapter are fundamental. They equip aspiring certified developers with the knowledge and insights needed to design, implement, and maintain sophisticated integration solutions that meet complex business requirements. This expertise is invaluable in an era where the ability to create seamless, efficient, and data-driven operations can be a significant competitive advantage for organizations.

Ultimately, mastering the integration of Business Central with other applications empowers developers to create comprehensive business solutions that drive real value. It enables the creation of unified systems that break down data silos, streamline workflows, and provide actionable insights. As businesses continue to digitize and automate their operations, the role of skilled integrators becomes increasingly crucial in shaping the future of work and commerce.

Key Takeaways

1. **Thorough Analysis Is Crucial**: Always begin integration projects with a comprehensive analysis of business needs and technical requirements to ensure alignment with organizational goals.

2. **Versatility in Integration Methods**: Business Central supports a wide range of integration techniques, from APIs and web services to low-code solutions and cloud functions. Choose the method that best fits your specific use case and technical environment.

3. **Data Integrity Is Paramount**: Implementing robust strategies for data synchronization and consistency is essential for maintaining reliable and trustworthy integrated systems.

4. **Best Practices Enhance Success**: Adhering to best practices in areas such as architecture design, security, performance optimization, and maintenance significantly improves the chances of integration success and long-term sustainability.

5. **Integration Is an Ongoing Process**: View integration as a continuous journey that requires ongoing attention, refinement, and adaptation to evolving business needs and technological advancements.

6. **Security Cannot Be an Afterthought**: Implement strong security measures from the outset, including proper authentication, authorization, and data protection strategies.

7. **Performance Matters**: Optimize integration performance through efficient API usage, asynchronous processing, and smart caching strategies to ensure responsive and scalable solutions.

8. **Testing Is Critical**: Implement comprehensive testing strategies, including automated tests and staging environments, to catch issues early and ensure reliable integrations.

9. **Documentation and Knowledge Sharing**: Maintain thorough documentation and foster knowledge sharing to support long-term maintenance and continuity of integration projects.

10. **Stay Informed and Adaptable**: Keep abreast of emerging technologies and integration trends to continuously improve and innovate in your integration approaches.

CHAPTER 5   INTEGRATION OF BUSINESS CENTRAL WITH OTHER APPLICATIONS

Exercise

1. Create the Customer Financial Insights App in Power Apps. This exercise is written to use the Alpine Ski House sample company from the US version of Business Central. You might need to make adjustments to the steps if you use the sample company from your country or region.

   Scenario

   Alpine Ski House has decided to create a small app for phone devices that provides financial insights about customers from Dynamics 365 Business Central. The goal is to equip their sales team with the most up-to-date financial information on their clients.

   As the IT manager at Alpine Ski House, you've been tasked with creating this app without involving external developers. You've chosen to build the app as a canvas app in Power Apps, leveraging the existing API for customer financial details in Business Central, which requires no coding.

Solution

1. Start with Power Apps.
2. Create a connection to Business Central.
3. Connect with the API in Business Central.
4. Change the name in the gallery.
5. Remove the ID field in the details card.
6. Test the app.
7. Save and share the app.

CHAPTER 6

Exam Preparation and Practice

Exam preparation and practice serves as an essential guide for aspiring Microsoft Dynamics 365 Business Central Developers preparing for the MB-820 certification exam. This comprehensive chapter is designed to equip candidates with a thorough understanding of the exam structure, effective study strategies, and practical exercises to enhance their readiness for this important career milestone.

The chapter begins by providing a detailed overview of the exam objectives and structure, giving candidates a clear picture of what to expect. It breaks down the six main skill areas assessed in the exam, including describing Business Central, installation and deployment, development using AL objects and AL Language, working with development tools, and integrating Business Central with other applications. This section also covers the types of questions candidates may encounter, the exam format, and the scoring system, emphasizing the importance of time management during the test.

Following this, the chapter delves into effective study strategies and resources. It offers guidance on creating a personalized study schedule, identifying and utilizing official Microsoft resources, and leveraging third-party study materials. The chapter also emphasizes the importance of hands-on practice with Business Central development and provides tips for effective note-taking and information retention, ensuring that candidates can make the most of their preparation time.

A significant portion of the chapter is dedicated to practice exercises and sample questions. This section offers a diverse set of questions covering all exam objectives, accompanied by detailed explanations for each answer. It also includes hands-on exercises that simulate real-world Business Central development scenarios, helping candidates apply their knowledge in practical situations. Strategies for approaching different question types, such as multiple-choice, case study-based, and hands-on tasks, are also provided to build confidence and improve exam performance.

The chapter concludes with invaluable tips for exam day readiness. It provides a pre-exam preparation checklist, strategies for managing exam anxiety, and techniques for effective time management during the test. Guidance on how to approach difficult questions is also included, along with advice on post-exam steps and how to continue developing one's career in Business Central development.

Throughout the chapter, the focus remains on practical, exam-oriented preparation. By working through this chapter, readers will not only prepare for the MB-820 exam but also deepen their understanding of Business Central development, viewing the certification process as a valuable learning experience that enhances their professional skills and career prospects.

Overview of MB-820 Exam Objectives and Structure

The MB-820 Microsoft Dynamics 365 Business Central Developer associate certification exam is designed to validate the skills and knowledge of professionals who develop, customize, and maintain solutions based on Dynamics 365 Business Central.

CHAPTER 6   EXAM PREPARATION AND PRACTICE

Exam Objectives

The exam covers six main skill areas, each focusing on critical aspects of Business Central development:

Skill area	Description	Key topics	Weightage
1. Describe Business Central	Understanding of Business Central's role and terminology	Business Central's relationship with Microsoft 365 and Dynamics 365 Industry terminology Core functionalities and modules	10–15%
2. Install, develop, and deploy for Business Central	Proficiency in setting up environments and managing the development lifecycle	Development environment setup Extension management Deployment processes AppSource publishing	10–15%
3. Develop by using AL objects	Ability to work with various AL objects to create and modify functionality	Tables and table extensions Pages and page extensions Reports and report extensions Codeunits Queries and XMLports	35–40%
4. Develop by using AL	Programming skills in AL Language	AL syntax and data types Control structures Error handling Best practices for efficient and maintainable code	15–20%

(*continued*)

CHAPTER 6   EXAM PREPARATION AND PRACTICE

Skill area	Description	Key topics	Weightage
5. Work with development tools	Proficiency in using associated development tools and technologies	Visual Studio Code and extensions AL Language extension Debugging tools Source control integration	10–15%
6. Integrate Business Central with other applications	Ability to connect Business Central with other systems	Integration with Microsoft Power Platform Web services and APIs Third-party application integration	10–15%

Exam Structure

While the exact format may vary, candidates can generally expect the following:

1. **Question Types**
   - Multiple-choice questions (majority)
   - Case study-based questions
   - Hands-on tasks in a simulated environment (performance-based items)
2. **Number of Questions**: Typically ranges from 40 to 60 questions
3. **Time Limit**: Usually 120-180 minutes
4. **Passing Score**: 700 out of 1000 points (subject to change)

CHAPTER 6   EXAM PREPARATION AND PRACTICE

5. **Adaptive Testing**: The exam may use adaptive testing techniques, adjusting question difficulty based on performance

6. **Coverage**: Questions are dynamically selected to cover all skill areas, ensuring a comprehensive assessment

7. **Scoring**: No penalty for incorrect answers; unanswered questions are marked as incorrect

8. **Results**: Provided immediately upon completion of the exam

Preparation Considerations

- Hands-on experience with Business Central development is crucial.
- Familiarity with all aspects of the Business Central platform, not just coding.
- Understanding of business processes and how they're implemented in Business Central.
- Regular practice with AL programming and object manipulation.
- Awareness of integration capabilities and limitations.

CHAPTER 6   EXAM PREPARATION AND PRACTICE

Study Strategies and Resources for MB-820 Exam

Preparing for the MB-820 Microsoft Dynamics 365 Business Central Developer Associate certification exam requires a structured approach and access to quality resources. This section outlines effective study strategies and provides a comprehensive list of resources to aid in your preparation.

1. Create a Study Plan

1.1 Assess Your Current Knowledge

- Take a practice test to identify areas of strength and weakness.
- Review the exam objectives and rate your confidence in each area.

1.2 Set a Timeline

- Determine your exam date.
- Work backwards to create weekly study goals.
- Allocate more time to areas where you need improvement.

1.3 Establish a Routine

- Set aside dedicated study time each day.
- Create a distraction-free study environment.
- Use time management techniques like the Pomodoro method (25 minutes of focused study followed by a 5-minute break).

2. Leverage Official Microsoft Resources
2.1 Microsoft Learn

- Complete the Dynamics 365 Business Central Developer Learning Path.
- Focus on modules directly related to exam objectives.

2.2 Microsoft Docs

- Study the Business Central Development documentation.
- Pay special attention to AL Language reference and best practices.

2.3 Official Exam Page

- Regularly check the MB-820 exam page for updates and changes to exam objectives.

3. Utilize Third-Party Resources
3.1 Books

- "Mastering Microsoft Dynamics 365 Business Central" by Stefano Demiliani
- "Programming Microsoft Dynamics 365 Business Central" by Roberto Stefanetti

3.2 Online Courses

- **Udemy**: Search for courses specifically targeting MB-820 exam preparation
- **Pluralsight**: Offers courses on Business Central development

3.3 Practice Tests

- **MeasureUp**: Offers official practice tests for MB-820
- **Whizlabs**: Provides practice exams and hands-on labs

4. Hands-On Practice

4.1 Set Up a Development Environment

- Install Visual Studio Code and the AL Language extension.
- Set up a sandbox environment for Business Central.

4.2 Work on Projects

- Create sample extensions covering different aspects of Business Central.
- Practice modifying existing functionality and creating new features.

4.3 Participate in Community Projects

- Contribute to open-source Business Central projects on GitHub.
- Participate in Microsoft's BusinessCentralApps repository.

5. Join Community and Discussion Forums

5.1 Microsoft Community

- Participate in Microsoft Dynamics 365 Community.
- Engage in discussions and problem-solving.

5.2 Stack Overflow

- Follow the dynamics-365-business-central tag.
- Answer questions to reinforce your knowledge.

5.3 LinkedIn Groups

- Join "Dynamics 365 Business Central Developers" group.
- Network with other professionals and share knowledge.

CHAPTER 6   EXAM PREPARATION AND PRACTICE

6. Effective Note-Taking and Review

6.1 Cornell Method

- Divide your notes into main points, details, and summary sections.
- Regularly review and synthesize your notes.

6.2 Mind Mapping

- Create visual representations of concepts and their relationships.
- Use tools like MindMeister or XMind.

6.3 Spaced Repetition

- Use flashcard apps like Anki to review key concepts regularly.
- Focus on areas where you struggle most.

7. Stay Updated

7.1 Follow Microsoft Blogs

- Subscribe to the Dynamics 365 Blog.
- Follow key Microsoft employees on social media.

CHAPTER 6   EXAM PREPARATION AND PRACTICE

7.2 Attend Webinars and Virtual Events

- Participate in Microsoft's virtual events and webinars.
- Attend community-organized online meetups and conferences.

MB-820 Exam: Practice Exercises and Sample Questions

This section provides scenario-based multiple-choice questions covering the main topics of the MB-820 exam. Each question is followed by four possible answers and an explanation of the correct answer.

1. Describe Business Central

Scenario: A client is considering implementing Dynamics 365 Business Central but is unsure about its integration capabilities with other Microsoft products.

Question: Which of the following best describes Business Central's integration with Microsoft 365?

A) Business Central can only integrate with Excel for data export.

B) Business Central has no integration with Microsoft 365 products.

C) Business Central integrates seamlessly with Outlook, allowing users to manage business interactions, invoices, and quotes directly from their email.

D) Business Central can only integrate with Power BI for reporting.

Correct Answer: C

Explanation: Business Central integrates seamlessly with various Microsoft 365 products, including Outlook. This integration allows users to manage business interactions, view customer information, and handle financial documents like invoices and quotes directly from their Outlook interface, enhancing productivity and streamlining workflows.

2. Install, Develop, and Deploy for Business Central

Scenario: You're setting up a new development environment for a Business Central project.

Question: Which of the following is NOT a required step when setting up a Business Central development environment?

A) Installing Visual Studio Code

B) Installing the AL Language extension

C) Setting up a Docker container with a Business Central instance

D) Installing SQL Server Management Studio

Correct Answer: D

Explanation: While Visual Studio Code, the AL Language extension, and a Business Central instance (often in a Docker container) are essential for a Business Central development environment, SQL Server Management Studio is not a requirement. Business Central uses SQL Server as its database, but direct database management is typically not part of the regular development workflow.

3. Develop by Using AL objects

Scenario: You need to create a new page in Business Central that displays a list of high-value customers.

CHAPTER 6   EXAM PREPARATION AND PRACTICE

Question: Which of the following AL object types would be most appropriate for this task?

A) Table
B) Codeunit
C) Report
D) Page

Correct Answer: D

Explanation: A Page object in AL is the most appropriate for creating a user interface that displays a list of data. In this case, a Page of type List would be ideal for showing high-value customers. Tables store the data, Codeunits contain business logic, and Reports are for printing or generating documents.

4. Develop by Using AL

Scenario: You're writing AL code to calculate a discount based on the order quantity. You want to ensure that the discount is never more than 50% of the Amount.

Question: Which of the following AL code snippets correctly implements this logic?

```
A) discount := amount * 0.1 * quantity; if discount > 50
   then discount := 50;
Copy
B) discount := MIN(amount * 0.1 * quantity, amount * 0.5);
C) if amount * 0.1 * quantity <= amount * 0.5 then discount
   := amount * 0.1 * quantity else discount := amount * 0.5;
D) discount := amount * 0.1 * quantity;
   CASE TRUE OF
     discount > amount * 0.5:
       discount := amount * 0.5;
   END;
```

Correct Answer: B

Explanation: Option B is the most concise and efficient way to calculate the discount while ensuring it doesn't exceed 50% of the amount. The MIN function compares the calculated discount (amount * 0.1 * quantity) with the maximum allowed discount (amount * 0.5) and returns the smaller value.

5. Work with Development Tools

Scenario: You're debugging an AL extension and need to step through the code to find an error.

Question: Which of the following Visual Studio Code features would be most helpful in this situation?

A) IntelliSense
B) Git integration
C) Breakpoints
D) Code snippets

Correct Answer: C

Explanation: Breakpoints are the most useful feature for debugging and stepping through code. They allow you to pause the execution of your code at specific points, examine variable values, and step through the code line by line to identify and fix errors.

6. Integrate Business Central with Other Applications

Scenario: A client wants to display real-time Business Central data in a Power BI dashboard.

Question: Which of the following methods would you recommend for integrating Business Central with Power BI?

A) Manually export data from Business Central and import it into Power BI daily

B) Use the built-in Power BI integration in Business Central to publish data and refresh it automatically

C) Create a custom API in Business Central and connect to it from Power BI

D) Use SQL Server Integration Services (SSIS) to transfer data between Business Central and Power BI

Correct Answer: B

Explanation: Business Central has built-in integration with Power BI, allowing users to publish data directly to Power BI and set up automatic refresh schedules. This method is the most straightforward and efficient way to create real-time dashboards with Business Central data in Power BI.

Tips for Exam Day Readiness: MB-820 Microsoft Dynamics 365 Business Central Developer

Being well-prepared for the day of your MB-820 exam can significantly impact your performance and reduce stress. Here are comprehensive tips to ensure you're ready for exam day:

1. Pre-exam Preparation

1.1 Verify Exam Details

- Double-check the exam date, time, and location (or online proctoring details).
- Ensure you have the correct identification documents required.

CHAPTER 6   EXAM PREPARATION AND PRACTICE

1.2 Technical Check (for Online Exams)

- Test your computer's compatibility with the exam software.
- Ensure a stable internet connection.
- Check your webcam and microphone are working properly.

1.3 Prepare Your Exam Environment

- Choose a quiet, well-lit space free from distractions.
- Inform family members or roommates about your exam to minimize interruptions.
- Clear your desk of all items except those allowed during the exam.

1.4 Mental Preparation

- Get a good night's sleep before the exam.
- Eat a balanced meal to maintain energy levels.
- Practice relaxation techniques like deep breathing or meditation.

2. On Exam Day

2.1 Arrive Early or Log in Early

- For in-person exams, arrive at least 30 minutes early.
- For online exams, start the check-in process 30 minutes before the scheduled time.

2.2 Manage Exam Anxiety

- Use positive self-talk to boost confidence.
- Remember your thorough preparation.
- Take deep breaths to stay calm and focused.

2.3 Read Instructions Carefully

- Take time to understand the exam structure and instructions.
- Note any specific guidelines for answering questions.

3. During the Exam

3.1 Time Management

- Read each question carefully, but be mindful of the clock.
- Allocate time for each section based on the number of questions.
- If stuck on a question, flag it and move on—return to it later if time permits.

3.2 Approach to Questions

- For multiple-choice questions
  - Read all options before selecting an answer.
  - Eliminate obviously incorrect answers to improve your odds.

- For scenario-based questions
  - Identify the key information in the scenario.
  - Consider how Business Central functionalities apply to the given situation.

3.3 Use the Process of Elimination

- If unsure, eliminate answers you know are incorrect.
- Make an educated guess from the remaining options.

3.4 Leverage Your Knowledge

- Draw on your hands-on experience with Business Central.
- Apply AL programming concepts to code-related questions.
- Consider best practices for Business Central development when answering scenario questions.

3.5 Stay Calm and Focused

- If you encounter a difficult question, take a deep breath and refocus.
- Remember that one challenging question doesn't define your overall performance.

CHAPTER 6 EXAM PREPARATION AND PRACTICE

4. After the Exam

4.1 Review Your Answers

- If time allows, review your answers.
- Pay special attention to flagged questions.
- Trust your initial instincts–only change an answer if you're certain it's wrong.

4.2 Submit with Confidence

- Double-check that you've answered all questions before submitting.
- Click submit with confidence, knowing you've done your best.

5. Post-exam Steps

5.1 Reflect on the Experience

- Make mental notes about the exam structure and types of questions.
- Identify areas where you felt confident and areas for improvement.

5.2 Next Steps

- If you pass, celebrate your achievement!
- If you don't pass, don't be discouraged. Use the experience to refine your study strategy for the next attempt.

5.3 Continuous Learning

- Regardless of the outcome, continue to deepen your knowledge of Business Central.

- Stay updated with the latest developments in the Dynamics 365 ecosystem.

Remember, the MB-820 exam is not just a test of your knowledge, but also of your ability to apply that knowledge in real-world scenarios. Stay calm, trust your preparation, and approach each question methodically. Good luck on your exam!

Conclusion

Preparing for the MB-820 Microsoft Dynamics 365 Business Central Developer associate certification exam is a comprehensive process that requires dedication, strategic planning, and hands-on practice. This chapter has provided you with a roadmap for success, covering the exam structure, effective study strategies, practice questions, and tips for exam day readiness.

Remember that earning this certification is not just about passing an exam; it's about demonstrating your proficiency in developing and maintaining Business Central solutions. The knowledge and skills you've gained through this preparation process will serve you well in your career as a Business Central developer, regardless of the exam outcome.

As you move forward, continue to engage with the Business Central community, stay updated with the latest developments, and apply your knowledge in real-world scenarios. Your journey as a Business Central developer doesn't end with certification—it's a continuous path of learning and growth in this dynamic field.

CHAPTER 6 EXAM PREPARATION AND PRACTICE

Key Takeaways

1. **Understand the Exam Structure**: Familiarize yourself with the six main skill areas covered in the MB-820 exam and the types of questions you'll encounter.

2. **Create a Comprehensive Study Plan**: Develop a structured study schedule that covers all exam objectives, allocating more time to areas where you need improvement.

3. **Utilize Diverse Learning Resources**: Leverage a combination of official Microsoft documentation, third-party study materials, and hands-on practice to reinforce your knowledge.

4. **Gain Practical Experience**: Set up a Business Central development environment and work on sample projects to apply your knowledge in real-world scenarios.

5. **Practice with Sample Questions**: Use practice exams and sample questions to familiarize yourself with the exam format and identify areas that need more focus.

6. **Develop Time Management Skills**: Practice answering questions within time constraints to improve your efficiency during the actual exam.

7. **Focus on AL Development**: Ensure you're comfortable with AL syntax, object types, and best practices for Business Central development.

8. **Understand Integration Capabilities**: Be well-versed in how Business Central integrates with other Microsoft products and third-party applications.

9. **Prepare for Exam Day**: Follow a structured approach to exam day preparation, including technical checks for online exams and strategies for managing exam anxiety.

10. **Continuous Learning**: View the certification process as part of your ongoing professional development in the Dynamics 365 ecosystem.

By internalizing these key takeaways and applying the strategies outlined in this chapter, you'll be well-equipped to tackle the MB-820 exam with confidence. Remember, thorough preparation is the key to success. Good luck on your certification journey!

Index

A

Adaptive testing techniques, 269
.alcpuprofile file, 158
AL, *see* Application Language (AL)
AL objects
    checklist
        comments and
            documentation, 119
        error handling, 120
        logging, 120
        maintainability, 122
        modularization and
            reusability, 119
        naming conventions, 119
        optimize data, 120
        security, 121
        testing/quality
            assurance, 121
        user experience, 121
        version control, 120
    codeunits, 123
    development
        data validation, 116
        documentation and
            comments, 114
        error handling, 115
        logging, 115
        maintainability, 117
        modularization and
            reusability, 113
        naming conventions, 114
        optimize data, 115
        practices, 117, 118
        security, 116
        testing/quality
            assurance, 116
        user experience, 116
        version control, 114
    extensions, 123
    pages, 86, 122
    queries, 123
    reports, 122
        create, 98, 100
        data items, 97
        design, 101, 102
        extensions, 100, 101
        triggers, 98
    tables, 122
        creating/modifying, 84
        design, 85, 86
        extensions, 84, 85
        fields, 81

INDEX

AL objects (*cont.*)
    keys, 82
    relations, 82
    triggers, 82
    types, 81
    XMLPorts, 123
AL programming language, 137
AL Test Runner, 141
APIs, *see* Application Programming Interfaces (APIs)
Application Language (AL), 5, 10, 13, 16, 18, 51, 79, 81, 139
    definition, 18
    vs. other languages, 19
    uniqueness, 19
Application Programming Interfaces (APIs), 230–231
AppSource submissions, 33, 55
Azure Active Directory, 147
Azure Application Insights, 148, 152, 159, 161, 175, 183–184, 187, 205, 225, 243
Azure Data Factory, 147
Azure DevOps, 57, 127, 140, 144, 152
Azure Functions, 207, 212, 215, 227, 228, 248, 259
    integration method for D365BC, 235, 236
    integration with Business Central, 212
Azure Load Testing, 185

B

Batch processing, 115, 120
    integration method for D365BC, 237–238
Branching strategy, 124–125, 143
Breakpoints, 51, 153–154, 161, 278
Business Central, 3–9
    database, 49
    extensibility, 48
    manage objects, 50
    numbering system, 49
    object types, 47, 48
    rules, 50
Business Central Administration Center, 141
Business Central API, 207, 214, 223
    integration method, 214
    integration with Business Central, 214
    RESTful interface, 214
Business Central development, 265–267, 269, 272, 282, 285
    MB-820 exam (*see* MB-820 certification exam)
Business Central extension, 139, 184, 186–190
Business Central integrations with Azure Functions, 212
    best practices for data synchronization and consistency, 244

INDEX

with Business Central API, 214
checklist (*see* E-commerce integration design)
data consistency, 239
data synchronization, 239
E-commerce integration for Worldwide Traders (*see* Worldwide Traders)
ensure data consistency
   conflict resolution, 242
   data validation and cleansing, 242
   master data management (MDM), 241
   version control and historization, 242
handling synchronization failures
   error logging and monitoring, 243
   manual intervention processes, 243
   retry mechanisms, 243
implement robust data synchronization, 245, 246
integration scenarios
   banking and financial services, 217
   business intelligence and reporting, 218
   CRM integration, 217
   e-commerce integration, 217
   human resources management, 218
   supply chain management, 217
   with Power Apps, 208, 209
   with Power Automate, 210
   with Power Pages, 216
   requirements for integration, 218, 219
   with REST Services, 211
   with Shopify, 214, 215
   synchronization methods (*see* Synchronization methods)
   with web services, 213
Business Central-specific performance tools for MB-820, 179
   AL-specific best practices, 181
   cloud performance considerations, 182
   Complex Business Central Extension, 186–190
   database performance optimization, 180, 181
   debug and optimize AL code, 190–192
   performance testing for extensions, 184, 185
   Performance Toolkit, 179, 180
   telemetry and performance testing, 192–194
Business Central-specific tools, 206

C

Card pages, 86, 87, 92, 132–135

INDEX

CardPart pages, 93
CI/CD, *see* Continuous Integration/
    Continuous
    Deployment (CI/CD)
Code reviews, 18, 116, 121, 125–126
Codeunits
    complete, 107, 108
    create, 103–105
    definition, 102
    development, 106
    events, 105
    features, 102, 103
Codeunit Web Services, 231
Cohesion, 118, 171
Commit practices, 125
Confirmation dialog pages, 94–95
Continuous Integration/
    Continuous Deployment
    (CI/CD), 57, 61, 127, 130,
    131, 140, 141, 143–144, 152
Continuous learning, 14, 18,
    284, 286
Coupling, 118, 171, 237, 247–248

D

Database Engine Tuning Advisor,
    181, 186
Data consistency, 28, 85, 86, 239,
    241–242, 246, 249
Data management,
    146–147, 248–249
Data synchronization, 208, 210,
    215, 233, 238–246

Dataverse, 67, 241
D365BC, *see* Dynamics 365
    Business Central (D365BC)
Debugging and troubleshooting
    techniques
    complex integration
        issue, 160–163
    Debugger in VS Code, 153–155
    error handling, 156, 157
    logging and tracing, 155, 156
    performance profiling, 157, 158
    telemetry and monitoring, 159
Deploying applications
    AI extensions, 54
    multiple tenants, 56
    postdeployment, 56
    preparation, 53, 54
    rollback strategy, 57
    tips, 57
    versions and updates, 55
Deployment strategies
    deployment process, 58, 59
    multitenant, 59, 60
    postdeployment activities, 60
    predeployment preparation, 58
    rollback strategy, 61
Design queries, 123
Developer tests, 11
Development environments
    Docker for local
        development, 150
    environment management
        access control, 147
        CI/CD pipelines, 143, 144

INDEX

    data management, 146, 147
    documentation, 148–150
    environment parity, 144, 145
    monitoring and logging, 148
    version control, 142, 143
  local development
    environment, 142
  production environment,
    142, 151
  Sandbox environment, 142, 150
  streamline multienvironment
    Development at
    TechnoGlobe Inc., 151, 152
Development tools
  AL Test Runner, 141
  Application Language (AL), 139
  Azure DevOps, 140
  Business Central
    Administration Center, 141
  Business Central extension, 139
  custom module, 23
  debugging and optimize AL
    Code, 195–202
  debugging and troubleshooting
    (*see* Debugging and
    troubleshooting
    techniques)
  deployment, 22
  Docker containers, 140
  performance optimization
    strategies (*see* Performance
    optimization)
  PowerShell, 140
  sandbox environment, 21
  source control systems, 22
  standalone development
    environments, 140
  utilization, development
    environments (*see*
    Development
    environments)
  VS code, 20, 21, 23, 128, 139
DevOps, 205
Docker containers, 137, 140, 142,
    204, 276
Document pages, 89–90, 92
Dynamics 365 Business Central
  (D365BC)
  automation of process, 28
  best practices for seamless
    integration
    continuous
      improvement, 253
    documentation and
      knowledge
      management, 252
    governance and support, 254
    performance optimization,
      250, 251
    robust architecture
      design, 247–249
    security and compliance,
      249, 250
    testing and quality
      assurance, 251
    thorough planning and
      analysis, 246, 247
  business efficiency, 12

INDEX

Dynamics 365 Business
  Central (D365BC) (*cont.*)
  checklist
    additional
      responsibilities, 18
    coding and
      implementation, 16
    collaboration and
      communication, 17
    continuous learning, 18
    deployment and
      maintenance, 17
    designing and architecting
      solutions, 16
    testing and debugging, 17
  collaboration
    integration streamlines, 8
    single platform, 8
  customized sales report
    coding, 11
    deployment, 12
    design and planning, 11
    developer tests, 11
    functional testing, 11
    gathers the requirements, 11
    UAT, 11
  data consistency, 28
  decision making
    advanced reporting/
      analytics, 7
    real-time data access, 7
  deployment strategy, 5
  designing solutions
    automated testing, 53
    deployment, 52
    development, 51
    documentation, 53
    testing, 52
    use version control, 53
  developer
    certification, 14
    coding and
      implementation, 13
    communication and
      collaboration, 14
    deployment and
      maintenance, 13
    designing and architecting
      solutions, 12
    quality assurance and
      debugging, 13
  extensions/customizations, 5
  features, 3
  financial management, 2
  fragmented systems, 27
  inconsistent data, 27
  increased efficiency
    automated workflow, 6
    integrated operations, 6
  integration techniques
    and methods
    APIs, 230, 231
    Azure Functions, 235, 236
    batch processing, 237, 238
    Event-Driven Architecture,
      236, 237
    Power Apps, 234

INDEX

    Power Automate, 232, 233
    Web services, 231, 232
manual process, 27
operations management, 4
with Power Pages, 216
project management, 4
real-time access, 28
real-time data, 27
responsibilities
    deployment and
        maintenance, 10
    design and architecture, 9
    implementing code, 10
    testing and debugging, 10
sales and service
    management, 3
scalability
    flexible deployment
        options, 7
    modular design, 8
Shopify, 214, 215
supply chain management, 3
unified platform, 28
upgrade
    assessment and planning, 15
    code refactoring, 15
    deployment, 15
    support and
        maintenance, 15
    testing, 15

E

E-commerce integration design

    architecture design, 255
    best practices
        implementation, 259
    compliance and legal
        considerations, 258
    data synchronization strategy
        customer information, 256
        inventory updates, 256
        order management, 256
        product information, 255
    data validation and
        integrity, 257
    deployment and
        maintenance, 258
    documentation and
        training, 258
    error handling and
        monitoring, 257
    future-proofing, 258
    integration method
        selection, 255
    security considerations, 256, 257
    testing strategy, 257
Enterprise resource planning
    (ERP), 2, 19, 24
Environment parity, 144–145
ERP, *see* Enterprise resource
    planning (ERP)
Error handling, 73, 101, 106, 113,
    115, 118, 120, 156–157, 161,
    196, 218, 225, 246, 248, 257
Event-Driven Architecture, 212
    integration method for
        D365BC, 236–237

INDEX

F
Functional testing, 11

G, H
Gitflow, 124, 143
GitHub Copilot, 80, 128–129, 174

I, J, K
Integration testing, 52, 226, 251, 257

L
launch.json file, 44, 158
List pages, 88
ListPart pages, 92
Logging, 115, 118, 120, 148, 152, 155–156, 160, 205, 218, 225

M
Managing sandbox environments, 32
Master data management (MDM), 241, 245
MB-820 certification exam, 266
    exam objectives, 267, 268
    exam structure, 268, 269
    post-exam steps, 283, 284
    practice exercises and sample questions
        Business Central, 275, 276
        development by using AL, 277, 278
        development by using AL objects, 276, 277
        install, develop and deploy for Business Central, 276
        integrate Business Central, 278, 279
        work with development tools, 278
    study strategies and resources
        create study plan, 270
        development environment, 272
        join community and discussion forums, 273
        note-taking and review, 274
        official Microsoft resources, 271
        participate in community projects, 273
        stay updated, 274, 275
        utilize third-party resources, 271, 272
        work on projects, 272
    tips for exam day readiness
        after exam, 283
        AL programming, 282
        approach to questions, 281, 282
        Business Central development, 282
        during exam, 281, 282
        on exam day, 280, 281

pre-exam preparation, 279, 280
process of elimination, 282
submit with confidence, 283
MDM, *see* Master data management (MDM)
MegaRetail Corp, 173
Merging branches, 126
Microsoft Flow, 210, 232–233
MindMeister, 274
Modularization, 106, 113, 118, 119

N

Namespaces
 declaring, 62
 directive, 63
 nested, 64
 objects, 64
 prefix/suffix, 64
 using keyword, 63
Nested namespaces, 64, 65

O

OData web services, 213, 231
OnSaveLinks, 181–182

P

Pages
 card, 87
 CardPart, 93
 confirmation dialog, 94, 95
 document, 89
 list, 88
 ListPart, 92
 role center, 89
 standard dialog, 95, 97
 types, 86
 worksheet, 91
Page Web Services, 231
Performance optimization
 application design, 171–173
 background processing, 168, 169
 caching strategies, 167, 168
 code optimization, 163–165
 optimize large-scale inventory management system, 173–178
 query optimization, 165, 166
Performance Toolkit, 179–180
Power Apps, 208, 259, 263
 integration method, 67–68, 71–72, 209
 integration method for D365BC, 234
 integration with Business Central, 209
Power Automate, 70, 72–73, 207, 224, 259
 cloud-based service, 210
 integration method, 68–69, 210
 integration method for D365BC, 232, 233
 integration with Business Central, 210

295

INDEX

Power Pages
    with D365BC, 216
    integration method, 216
    as Power Apps
        Portals, 216
Power Platform
    BI integration, 65–67
    Dont's, 70
    Do's, 69, 70
    postintegration, 74
    power apps integration, 67, 68, 71, 72
    power automate integration, 68, 69, 72, 73
    power BI integration, 71
    virtual agents integration, 73
PowerShell, 140, 179
Pre-exam preparation checklist, 266
Production environment, 13, 21, 52, 58, 59, 115, 142, 151, 155, 159
Pull requests, 125–126

Q

Queries
    AL code, 111, 112
    concepts, 108
    create, 109
    joins/filters, 110, 111
Query Store, 180

R

RBAC, *see* Role-based access control (RBAC)
Registered Solution Program (RSP), 49
Representational State Transfer (REST) services, 207, 211, 214, 230
    integration method, 211
    integration with Business Central, 211
REST services, *see* Representational State Transfer (REST) services
Role-based access control (RBAC), 147, 249
Role center pages, 89
RSP, *see* Registered Solution Program (RSP)

S

Sales Calculator codeunit, 195
Sandbox environment, 21, 24, 25, 32, 53, 55, 76, 142, 145, 150
Semantic versioning, 126
SetLoadFields, 181, 186
Shopify, 214, 220–223, 227, 256, 258
    integration method, 215
    integration with D365BC, 215
Simple extension, 77
SOAP web services, 213

Standalone development
　　environments, 140–141
Standard dialog pages, 95–97
Synchronization methods
　　batch synchronization, 240
　　hybrid approach, 240, 241
　　real-time synchronization,
　　　　239, 240

T

Tagging, 126
TechnoGlobe Inc., 151–153
Telemetry, 159, 161, 179, 187, 189,
　　192–194, 197–204
Test queries, 113, 123
Time management, 265, 266, 270,
　　281, 285

U

UAT, *see* User acceptance
　　testing (UAT)
Unit Testing, 52, 116, 121, 226
User acceptance testing (UAT), 11,
　　32, 52, 226
User Communication, 57, 74

V

VCS, *see* Version control
　　system (VCS)
Version control, 22, 23, 53, 55, 80,
　　114–115, 120, 124, 128,
　　142–143, 242

Version control system (VCS), 55,
　　114, 120, 124, 128, 143
　　backup and recovery, 127
　　branching strategy, 124, 125
　　CI/CD pipelines, 127
　　code reviews, 125
　　commit practices, 125
　　documentation and
　　　　training, 128
　　merging branches, 126
　　pull request, 125
　　source, 124
　　tagging and versioning, 126
Versioning, 126
Visual Studio Code (VS Code), 20,
　　21, 23, 128, 137–139,
　　143, 278
　　AL, 35
　　　　Docker images, 38
　　　　install, 36, 37
　　　　post install, 37
　　　　prerelease versions, 38, 39
　　　　test and debug, 37, 38
　　components, 35
　　extensions, 34
　　features, 34
　　install, 34
　　steps for installation
　　　　configure project, 44, 46
　　　　deploy and run, 47
　　　　download, 39
　　　　install AL, 40–42
　　　　set up development
　　　　　　environment, 41–44

INDEX

Visual Studio
  Code (VS Code) (*cont.*)
    sign up, 39
    tips for enhancing, 47
VS Code, *see* Visual Studio Code (VS Code)

W

Web-based tool, 141
Web services, 207, 213, 259, 261
  integration method, 213
  integration method for D365BC, 231–232
  integration with Business Central, 213
  SOAP and OData, 213
Worksheet pages, 91
Worldwide Traders, 219, 220, 228
  Business Central and Shopify integration, 220
  business challenge, 220
  change management, 229
  continuous monitoring and optimization, 229
  data mapping complexity, 229
  integration requirements
    customer data, 222
    financial reconciliation, 223
    inventory synchronization, 220, 221
    order management, 221
    product information, 222
  integration solution architecture
    Azure Functions, 224, 225
    Business Central API, 223
    challenges faced and solutions, 227
    error handling and monitoring, 225–227
    Power Automate flows, 224
    webhooks, 225
  outcomes and benefits, 228
  real-time inventory updates, 229
  scalability planning, 229
  system landscape, 219
  user training, 229

X, Y, Z

XMind, 274

GPSR Compliance
The European Union's (EU) General Product Safety Regulation (GPSR) is a set of rules that requires consumer products to be safe and our obligations to ensure this.

If you have any concerns about our products, you can contact us on

ProductSafety@springernature.com

In case Publisher is established outside the EU, the EU authorized representative is:

Springer Nature Customer Service Center GmbH
Europaplatz 3
69115 Heidelberg, Germany

www.ingramcontent.com/pod-product-compliance
Lightning Source LLC
LaVergne TN
LVHW010337260326
834688LV00036B/747